The Rt Revd Dr Emma Ineson is Bishop to the Archbishops of Canterbury and York, Chair of the Lambeth Conference Working Group and Central Chaplain to the Mothers' Union. She was Bishop of Penrith from 2019 to 2021. Prior to that, Emma was Principal of Trinity College Bristol, where she taught practical theology, leadership and spirituality, and previously Chaplain at the Lee Abbey community. She is married to Mat, who is a leadership enabler for CPAS. They have two adult children and two black dogs.

FAILURE

What Jesus said about sin,
mistakes and messing stuff up

Emma Ineson

First published in Great Britain in 2022

Society for Promoting Christian Knowledge
36 Causton Street
London SW1P 4ST
www.spck.org.uk

British Library Cataloguing-in-Publication Data
A catalogue record for this book is available from the British Library

ISBN 978–0–281–08784–6
eBook ISBN 978–0–281–08785–3

1 3 5 7 9 10 8 6 4 2

Typeset by Fakenham Prepress Solutions, Fakenham, Norfolk NR21 8NL
First printed in Great Britain by Clays Ltd

eBook by Fakenham Prepress Solutions, Fakenham, Norfolk NR21 8NL

Produced on paper from sustainable sources

Contents

Foreword

Some time ago, I was in a car with a very senior executive. Stuck in bad traffic, talking about this and that, suddenly he said: 'Do you ever feel that you might be a fake, that what everyone sees is not the reality? I feel it all the time.' I told him that I felt the same, and we talked about impostor syndrome.

He had given voice to something that almost all of us experience. Only a very few people feel that they are worthy of success. But we have learnt that failure is a dirty word and, if it happens, we must blame someone else to avoid being 'found out' – or even admitting to ourselves that we have gone wrong.

A few years ago, there was an article about former President Donald Trump. He had a habit of separating people into 'winners' and 'losers'. He had promised that, if he was elected, Americans would be winners so often that they would get fed up with winning. But he derided people he didn't like as 'losers'. As I remember, the article suggested this spoke to a key problem, not just in his presidency, but in society as a whole: we have learnt to see failure, which is inevitable, as unconscionable, a statement of our very worth and value. And this means our only option is to be a 'winner', to keep proclaiming our successes, even in the face of facts that say otherwise. What was needed was some sort of societal coming to terms with failure.

In the Church of England, when I was training for ordained ministry, someone told me off for speaking of success and failure. Many times, when there have been big decisions to make, people have said, 'Don't set a target; we might not meet it.'

Yet that is not the way the Bible, or Christian history, or human experience, deals with the reality of life, or of our world. In politics it is said that 'every political career ends in failure'. The Bible faces the reality of 'failed' lives again and again. Look at the story of Jacob who, at the end of his life, describes it as short and hard. Or of Joseph, whose work is undone when there is a ruler who forgot him. Or of the people of Israel in the time of the Judges. Or of Psalm 88, or of Jesus' disciples, or of Paul in 2 Corinthians 1. Failure is human, universal and inevitable. The question is what we do with it and, even more importantly, what God does with it in partnership with us.

There is a maxim known as Kanter's law, after the Harvard Business School professor who developed it: 'In the middle, everything looks like failure.' In the middle, in the liminal place that Christians inhabit, before the coming of Christ in victory, a lot of things might look like failure to us. But if we are judged – or judge others – only by when we fail, then all of us will be consumed with a sense of despair. Even the most spectacular disappointments and failures, public or private, are not the end of the story. The end of the story is written by God.

Emma Ineson, having written a superb book on ambition, has now written a superb book on failure. She is humorous, realistic and absolutely not judgemental. She faces the issues of failure, perceived, deceived and real. She brings us face to face with God who knows what a failure is and is not, and whose gracious love overwhelms the greatest failures. God set a different scale for measuring success and failure, and the Bible is above all a story of failure redeemed, failure forgiven, failure overcome in resurrection and merciful judgement.

This a very good book, rooted in Scripture; it will disturb us when we are too comfortable, and comfort us when we are too disturbed. It calls us to let God be the judge, and calls us to take comfort in his merciful and hope-filled judgement.

+ + *Justin Cantuar*
Lambeth Palace, London

Acknowledgements

This book is dedicated to all those who sit in the seats and pews of churches up and down the length and breadth of the country, week by week, listening to sermons, singing songs and hymns, kneeling (or sitting) to pray, breaking bread, listening to the notices, drinking tea from pale green cups – and then go out into the world to try to live for Jesus in schools, workplaces, universities, hospitals, prisons, businesses, factories, shops, farms and homes. Sometimes you feel you get it right, and it is glorious. Sometimes you fail and mess it up. But the point is that God loves you, whichever it is this week. So this book is for all of us who feel like failures but never are in the eyes of God. It is also dedicated to clergy and church leaders on whom the pressure to 'succeed' in various ways is immense and yet who are human, too, and so feel the pain of failure keenly. They are the real heroes. I have written this book at a time when the Church of England especially is wrestling with what it is here for, and so also with what it means to fail and what to do about it. I wish to thank all with whom I have worked over the years – in committees, working parties, synods, bishops' meetings, councils – to see the Church of England becoming more recognizably the kind of Church Christ died to create. I would like to thank all at SPCK who have been so supportive in encouraging me to write *Failure* as the sequel to *Ambition* (SPCK, 2019), especially Sam Richardson, Alison Barr, Michelle Clark and

Acknowledgements

Rima Devereaux. Any errors are my own (and probably quite appropriate in a book on failure). As ever, my family has been the bedrock of everything and I am immensely proud of and grateful to them all, especially Mat, Toby, Molly and George.

1

Why I wrote this book – or 'success and failure revisited'

I would say in my prayers – I may be this terrible person, this failure as an Archbishop, whatever it is, but I know you know me better than I know myself and you still love me. And by that I am held.
Justin Welby, Archbishop of Canterbury, interview with Jennifer Meierhans, BBC News online (2022)

In 2019, I wrote a book about ambition and how Christians might understand success.[1] It was a good book. It included lots of inspiring stuff about how not to be afraid of ambition and how to channel your passions and desires to the best ends for the furtherance of the kingdom of God.

And then a global pandemic struck.

Almost overnight the world fell on its face, and everything we thought we knew about how to do ordinary things, like go to work, mix with other people and simply stay alive, was turned upside down. Trains stopped running. Bins weren't collected. Everything closed. I recall some of the early days of the COVID-19 pandemic when I wondered whether or not I'd be able to buy the food for my family for the coming week. I was not used to this. I am fortunate enough never to have lived through war or famine and had been comfortably accustomed to being able to do, and get, what I wanted, whenever I wanted. But all that changed on 23 March 2020. And we had it relatively easy in the UK. We may not have been able to buy toilet roll for a short while, but at least we had hospitals, and mostly enough food, and, eventually, access to the vaccines. That's more than many in the world were able to say.

The COVID pandemic has had a profound impact on the Church. As a bishop in Cumbria, in the north-west of England, I had been due to go and preach at a local church the Sunday following the first lockdown announcements. That and every service for the foreseeable future was cancelled. I offered to send them my sermon notes to read at home instead. Very quickly an impressive effort was mounted to take church services online and once we discovered Zoom, there was no stopping us. Even the remotest churches in Cumbria found that services could be held quite effectively online. And meetings. Lots and lots of meetings. So we 'pivoted' and we coped and we soldiered on.

Lockdowns came and went. Numbers of COVID cases rose and fell, masks were worn and hands sanitized, and the Church learnt how to be the virtual Church. Ambition and success began to look very different.

Counting things took on a whole new hue too. Whereas previously we may have thought about the growth of the Church in terms of 'bums on pews', during the pandemic that wasn't so straightforward as bums weren't allowed on pews. Or anywhere in the building. How do you count the number of people 'at' your service when they are all tiny squares on a screen or fleeting views on YouTube? What if their Internet goes down in the middle of the service, do you still count them? (There was one glorious Sunday morning in May 2020 when the whole Internet crashed and there were rumours that Christians had broken it with their worship.) And what if there is one person who is officially 'logged on' but another is listening in from the next room? And how long does someone need to linger over your Facebook livestream for it to count as 'attending'?

Did the Church do better and grow during COVID or did it do worse and decline? No one really seemed to know. What we do know is that all the adapting, changing, caring took its toll on everyone. The sheer pressure of having constantly to adapt in the face of an ever-changing threat and the responsibility of keeping family, friends, communities and congregations safe was a heavy burden to bear.

We were promised a 'new normal' but, since the pandemic (can we even say that?), things seem to have become more uncertain, not less. The new Prime Minister in the UK, Liz Truss (or perhaps someone else by the time you are reading this), cannot fail to be aware of the huge task facing her as the cost of living and energy crises bite, the challenges facing the NHS mount up and the worldwide effects of the war in Ukraine threaten the lives, livelihoods and way of life of so many. Also, we have been grieving the death of our much loved and respected monarch, Queen Elizabeth II, who was on the throne for more than 70 years. The many people who laid flowers in her memory in the royal parks, the hundreds of thousands of people who queued through the night to see her coffin lying in state and the billions of people who watched her funeral on television did so because they mourned the loss of Her Late Majesty herself – who she was and what she did – but also, I suspect, because they grieve the passing of what she represented – stability, self-sacrifice, service.

Sometimes it can seem as though everything is crumbling around us.

We need to look failure full in the face. That is partly because it is looking us full in the face all the time. We can't escape from it. Every day each one of us will fail in myriad small and large ways. Every. Single. Day. The teabag left in the cup too long, the bus missed by leaving it too late to get to the bus stop, the deadline missed because an email was overlooked, the employee who fails to meet a target this month, the exam failed because of a question missed out and left unanswered, the family left unhoused because someone made an administrative error, the patient who died because someone misdiagnosed an illness, the monuments erected to people who made great wealth but did so on the backs of enslaved people, the country invaded because a neighbouring leader becomes paranoid about a regional imbalance of power.

I have wondered what qualifies me to write this book. I have not experienced many of the troubles and failures that blight the lives of many people around the world. I have been fortunate enough to have had, thus far, a happy and healthy life. I am a well-educated, white, middle-class, middle-aged, heterosexual woman, living a relatively comfortable life, in a Western city. I have a family I adore and who loves me. I have a job I enjoy most of the time and a challenging but fulfilling vocation as a bishop in the Church of England. I have not experienced too many setbacks. Yet my life, although blessed in many ways, has had its fair share of griefs and disappointments, some of which I will talk about in this book. I, like many others, live with a constant worry that I may not be quite good enough, I don't come up to scratch, I may make a fatal mistake at any moment. What if I get it wrong? I worry daily about the impact of failure on myself, my family, the Church I love. Will my children and their generation survive what we are doing to our climate? Will the elderly and vulnerable in our communities be able to heat their homes this winter? Will my friends in other parts of the Anglican Communion be able to find access to the vaccine, provision for themselves and their families, education, health care? Will the Church be able to recover its confidence in the gospel of Christ and build on the opportunities that present themselves after the COVID pandemic and reverse the decline of generations? Will the Church of England be able to stay together as we make decisions about our response to LGBTQI+ people, and decide whether or not to embrace equal marriage or the blessing of same-sex relationships?

What qualifies me to write about failure? I am a member of the human race.

The question is not 'Will there be failure?' but, rather, 'When there is failure, what will we do about it and what will we do with it?' Not all failure is terminal or hurts other people. But some is and does. So the question is, how do we learn to get better at making better mistakes? How do we make the kinds of mistakes that are safe, contained and lead to learning about what went wrong, so as to avoid making them again or, worse still, making larger, more painful mistakes?

My current job is working for the leader of a large Christian denomination, supporting the ministries of the Archbishops of Canterbury and York, and the bishops of the Church of England. The Archbishop of Canterbury is the spiritual leader of the Church of England and so is an instrument of the Anglican Communion of 85 million people worldwide. A large part of my working life, therefore, is spent dealing with failures.

When things go wrong and people have exhausted local avenues, they tend to get in touch with the Archbishop of Canterbury, in the hope that those things can be Sorted Out. Many of the letters about those things land on my desk. The daily postbag is a sorry litany of situations in which someone has hurt someone else and someone has failed. A churchwarden accuses the vicar of bullying, a cathedral clergy chapter has ruptured into factions, a bishop is accused of dealing badly with someone's complaint. Each one of the letters therefore represents failure of one kind or another – mostly the failure of ordinary people to treat one another with care, dignity and respect.

Then there are the more serious allegations of misconduct, which end up being handled under what is called the Clergy Discipline Measure (CDM). The CDM, passed by the General Synod in 2003, was brought in to deal with allegations of misconduct made against clergy in the Church of England. Anyone can submit a form (on the Church of England website), which is sent to the local bishop or the Archbishop. The form is then sent to a lawyer to decide whether or not the person is eligible to bring such an allegation and whether or not it is serious enough to warrant further exploration and investigation.

Allegations can take many months, even years, to resolve, rarely to the satisfaction of everyone. It's a blunt instrument in which all issues are dealt with in generally the same way, using the same process, from complaints that someone looked at someone else in a funny way after a church service to the most serious allegations of wrongdoing and harm to children and vulnerable adults. Additionally, when allegations are made under the CDM, they can take longer than necessary and complex processes are involved, because people are afraid to admit early on, 'Yes, I made a mistake. I am very sorry,' for fear of what will happen. It is sometimes possible for a respondent (the person against whom the allegation is made) to admit the wrongdoing and accept a lesser penalty – most likely what's called a 'rebuke' – but people are afraid to admit to shortcomings for fear of unknown, more severe outcomes, and so the process goes on for a longer time. If we had a more balanced approach to mistakes and failures, much of the pain and frustration of these complex legal processes could be avoided. Thankfully, the system is now under review, which is just as well, because what the CDM does not do very well is enable us as the Church to approach failure in a careful and nuanced way.

In my role I also witness what happens when things go badly wrong. Very badly wrong. In the Church of England, we have a large department that exists purely to acknowledge, investigate and prevent further abuse of children and adults who are vulnerable. The department exists because the Church has not always been a safe place and people have been treated most dreadfully. There have been times when those in authority have not acted to stop the abuse and people have been harmed more than they would otherwise have been, had action been taken earlier and more decisively or sensitively or carefully. Now, many people in the Church, and most especially its senior leaders, are rightly held more closely to account and trained and equipped to spot abuse or the potential for abuse before it happens and, if it does, to know how to deal with it effectively. The department exists to acknowledge past failure and prevent it happening in the future.

There have been times when the Church has either been complicit in institutional and societal failure or has itself failed, which has sometimes affected whole groups of people. The report into racism in the Church of England, 'From lament to action',[2] catalogues a series of failures in the way in which the Church has treated Minority Ethnic and Global Majority Heritage peoples, denying them a voice and a presence at the tables of authority and failing to give honour and dignity to all. The report calls for the Church to, 'repent of racial sin, turn away from racism and be reconciled, so that we may all experience the love of God'.[3] Other groups – women, LGBTQI+ people, people with disabilities, for example – have also been the victims of the Church's failure to welcome and include everyone, to see all people as equal and dearly loved by God and to act in accordance with that belief.

The Archbishop of Canterbury has apologized on several occasions on behalf of the Church of England for its failings. On a visit to Canada, he apologized to Indigenous communities whose children had been placed in so-called 'residential schools', some of which were run by the Church of England. He said:

> I am here today with a heart filled with a sense of darkness, shame and sadness, to acknowledge the hurt done to your people. To apologise for the damage caused to your communities . . . and to recognise the grievous sins of the Church of England in its historic form against the First Nations, the Inuit and the Métis people of Canada.[4]

The Archbishop is not directly responsible for the crimes of the past, but he apologized on behalf of those who, long ago, were complicit in failing a whole generation of Indigenous peoples, the effects of which continue to be keenly felt today. What is to be our stance in relation to the failings of our Church, our society, humanity as a whole?

These kinds of failures are large and, rightly, elicit much attention from the media and others. Most failures, though, go unnoticed by all except those most affected. Sometimes it seems as though we do failure well. We acknowledge, we apologize, we repent, we learn. Other times we do not. Sometimes it seems as though life is just one long series of failures and we can begin to feel weary in our very souls. The trouble is, we can never escape from failure. We can try very hard to do better all the time, but the fact is, failure is here to stay, because sin is here to stay. Ever since Eve said to Adam in the garden of Eden, 'Hey, try some of this!', human beings have been failing people.

In the UK, we appear to be living at the tail end of the COVID pandemic. After several waves, variants and lockdowns, the approach, here in the UK at least, is to 'learn to live with the virus'. There are no longer any restrictions on activity, meetings or movement, but people are still encouraged to self-isolate if they test positive, although that is not enforced. Few now wear masks on public transport or in confined spaces. Seven out of ten of us have had COVID. The most vulnerable are offered boosters, and drugs to lessen the effects of the disease should they catch it. We're learning to live with COVID. Perhaps the reality of failure is something like that. Try hard as we might to limit, escape or avoid failure, we cannot dodge it completely or eradicate it from our midst. Perhaps, instead, the knack is to learn to live with it, to take different approaches to different kinds of failure, to attempt to avoid the worst kinds and to find ways to mitigate its effects. As Joe Moran says:

> We can no more escape failure than protect ourselves entirely from any other contagion, and for the same reason: no one ever made themselves immune to other people. We like to see ourselves as sovereign entities that succeed or fail under their own steam. Failure is the virus we hope never to catch, but it has too many strains for us to escape it indefinitely. Sooner or later in the chickenpox party of life, everyone catches failure from everyone else.[5]

Life is lived with a constant feeling of failure. Every day when I look in the mirror, I see the ways in which my body is failing and the aspects of my physical appearance that I am less than delighted about. Every time I go to a meeting, I am aware of the dynamics of relating in the room, which are usually less than perfect because the participants are human beings. Every time I open my email inbox, I wonder what has failed now and who will be writing to me about it. Every time I go to a church service, I am mindful of what doesn't go right or how things might be better or how many people are not there. Every time I turn on my television, or open my news app, I see the failures of the world enacted on a global scale. Even the most supposedly 'successful' people must be aware of all this too? Failure is the wallpaper of life, so we'd better get used to it. The Turner Prize-winning artist and cultural activist Lubaina Himid advises 'dancing with failure, taking failure home, giving failure a cup of coffee and ending up in bed with failure'.[6]

Looking failure full in the face is a good idea from the perspective of organizational health too. Evidence shows that an organization which embraces the reality of failure and tries not to avoid it completely (for that is not possible), but to learn from it when it happens, is likely to be an organization where people are unafraid to take risks and greater progress is made as a result.

Amy Edmondson, a professor at Harvard Business School, has made it her life's work to study failure and to help organizations become better at dealing with it. The biggest problem, she says, is fear of failure. A culture that asks immediately, when something goes wrong, 'Whose fault is this and how should they be punished?' is a culture in which people will be afraid to risk trying anything new at all for fear it will go wrong and they will be blamed if it fails. If instead the culture is to encourage risk-taking and, therefore, the right kind of mistake-making – not to hide failure but recognize that everyone fails sometimes, failure need not be final and all failure can be used as a tool for learning and improvement – that is an organization where appropriate risks can be taken and progress will result. Edmondson says, 'Only leaders can create and reinforce a culture that counteracts the blame game and makes people feel both comfortable with and responsible for surfacing and learning from failures.'[7]

All this failure stuff is invariably lived out in the public glare, most often on social media. We human beings have a morbid fascination with failures, errors, mistakes and disasters. How often do we see traffic jams caused not by the accident on the motorway itself but by people slowing down on the other side of the road to gawp at the wreckage? When a public figure falls from grace the 'Twitterati' are quick to jump in with their own words of opprobrium, horror and indignation that such a person should have done such a thing, or else that such a person should be accused in this way, depending on their viewpoints. All this does not make for a nuanced approach to failure. A book published by the School of Life ('an organisation built to help us find calm, self-understanding, resilience and connection – especially during troubled times') entitled *On Failure* highlights the problem:

The internet has become an eternal charge sheet and bulletin board of every human being's record of disgrace, failure and idiocy. Twenty years after an infraction, the internet still reminds everyone about what we did and how others judged it – and the misdemeanour is as shocking and disappointing as it ever was.[8]

I recall that, when I was appointed to one post, someone whom I had barely met did a trawl of my background on the Internet and alighted on something I'd done (adding my signature to a letter) several years ago that I would not do now, for a variety of reasons that I would be very happy to explain to you were we to sit down and have a cup of coffee together. That person wrote a blog about it, defining me by that one small but significant action, overlooking anything of merit or otherwise I may have done before or since. It becomes more and more difficult to move on from our failures, or even the things we have done that are inadvisable or we would do differently now, or that we regret or have learnt from, because there is a permanent record of them on the Internet. God may take your sins and misdemeanours and put them in the deepest sea, but anyone with a search engine can fish them out again and serve them to you for breakfast.

What, then, should we do with failure? How do we live with failure, rather than expect to avoid it and make it all go away? There are many, many books written about failure. Most of them seem to suggest that failure is simply another step on the pathway to success. They have titles such as, *From Failure to Success: Everyday habits and exercises to build mental resilience and turn failures into successes, Failure Is Not Final: Motivational truths and strategies to cultivate success, Chasing Failure: How falling short sets you up for success, How to Fail at Almost Everything and Still Win Big: Kind of the story of my life* and *Adapt: Why success always starts with failure.* All very . . . motivational. *New York Times* bestselling author John C. Maxwell in his book, *Failing Forward: Turning mistakes into stepping stones for success*, recognizes failure as a natural and inevitable part of life – 'Everybody fails, errs and makes mistakes'[9] – yet the book frames failure as something that is inevitable on the road to success: 'Failure is simply a price we pay to achieve success.'[10]

This book aims to ask some questions about failure. What is it? How do we live well with it? What does God think about it? What do people think about the Church and failure? How do Christians think about failure? What happens when your get up and go has got up and gone, your energy to learn from failure is at its lowest ebb and failure seems to be the default for humanity? How do we live well with that? This book is intended to be read alone or with others or in groups, during Lent or at other times of the year – any time when failure may be possible. Lent is a good time to read it, though, because it's the season when we're supposed to examine ourselves and see where we're lacking.

There is a neglected liturgy in the Church of England, from the Book of Common Prayer, called, 'A commination or denouncing of God's anger and judgements against sinners', which involves 'certain prayers to be used on the first day of Lent, and at other times, as the ordinary shall appoint'.[11] I am not surprised that it is not often used, because it lays out in fairly bald terms all the ways in which human beings fail, sin, turn against God and generally hurt themselves and one another. It includes such wonders as confession by the person who 'removeth his neighbour's land-mark' or 'maketh the blind to go out of his way' or 'smiteth his neighbour secretly', as well as the 'unmerciful, fornicators, and adulterers, covetous persons, idolaters, slanderers, drunkards, and extortioners'. The liturgy begins with the words:

> Now seeing that all they are accursed (as the prophet David beareth witness) who do err and go astray from the commandments of God; let us (remembering the dreadful judgement hanging over our heads, and always ready to fall upon us) return unto our Lord God with all contrition and meekness of heart; bewailing and lamenting our sinful life, acknowledging and confessing our offences, and seeking to bring forth worthy fruits of penance.[12]

It is, perhaps, a little harsh and obtuse for most of our sensibilities these days, but it is helpful to remember the facts: we are sinful, fallen, failing people. We remember, too, the fact that God is a merciful God, and the service ends, thankfully, with the words, 'For thou art a merciful God, full of compassion, long-suffering, and of great pity.'

Just no removing your neighbour's landmark, OK?

Lent is a great time to think about our failures, but let's be careful how we approach this. During Lent, quite rightly, we bring our failures to mind and to the attention of a loving God who is always readier to forgive us than we are to repent. Sometimes, though it's tempting to treat Lent itself as something that we should be hugely successful at. I may try really hard to give up chocolate or swearing, and find myself very smug if I get to the end of a week without indulging in either. Alternatively, I may become despondent if I happen to slip up in the scrupulousness of the spiritual disciplines I have set myself. One writer says:

> I . . . wonder if a certain sense of failure during Lent is actually a good thing. In part, it reminds us that Lent is not a home renovation show. The primary goal of the season is not self-improvement; we are not here to fix up our own personal backsplash. We are trying to open ourselves to a deeper relationship with our friend and savior, Jesus.[13]

Above all, Lent is a time when we are encouraged to turn to God and God's word in the Bible and allow it to be reflected in our own lives to enable us to see ourselves as we really are. The problem is that the Bible is not the first place many people turn to today when looking for solutions to the problem of failure or even simply for comfort. The School of Life book *On Failure* laments:

> The man from Nazareth certainly understood suffering. And yet, for so many of us, the book

ultimately doesn't work, because we cannot believe in the beatific solutions being proffered. We are in biblical agony, yet godless. We are Job without even someone to question.[14]

We say that we should embrace failure and learn from it, but the story of God and his people is rarely one in which abject failure is turned into rip-roaring success. The Bible reframes what we think of as success and failure. The story we see most commonly is apparent success followed by failure and eventual redemption, but not in the ways originally expected. The success of creation – the pinnacle of which is humankind – is followed by the failure of the fall and banishment from the garden. The success of the flight from Egypt is followed by forty years of failure and wandering in the desert. The success of the Law being given to Moses on the mountaintop is followed by the failure of God's people to make do with anything other than a golden calf to worship. The success of the promised land is followed by the failure of exile. The success of successful King David (giant slayer – yay!) is followed by his own moral failure. The success of Jesus' ministry is followed by apparent failure on the cross. The success of God's Holy Spirit being poured out on all people is followed by the story of the Church being persecuted and scattered. The success of Pentecost is followed by 2,000 years of the fallible Church dividing and splitting and sinning and failing, even as it grows and spreads.

Is failure really something you encounter on the road to success or is it more often the other way round? Rather than seeing failure as the path to success, maybe we ought to see it instead as part of the weft and weave of life, part of the texture of our existence. We can ask what we will learn from it, of course, but perhaps more than that, we ought to accept it, reflect on it, think carefully about it and aim to fail well. Rather than asking how we get through it, instead we could ask what God is doing in and through it.

The past few years have caused us to shift our views on what constitutes success and failure. We have reimagined success. Perhaps we've lowered our expectations a little and now feel more comfortable living in the mess. It's acceptable for parents to collect their children from school in their pyjamas and I wear Crocs for most of my Zoom meetings. At one point during the pandemic, the people viewed as really successful, our heroes, were not bankers and stockbrokers, but key workers – bin collectors, delivery drivers, front-line health care workers. They were the people who kept us going and we applauded them on our doorsteps.

Perhaps it's time to rethink success and failure.

For discussion

1 How have the global and national events of the past few years affected your attitude to and experience of failure?
2 What kinds of failure are you most aware of at the moment, in your own life and that of others?
3 In what ways does society's judgement of failure influence you?

2

What is failure?

The pressure to succeed has a lot to do with why people overstep the line. It is a peculiar weakness of Western culture where we have made a fetish of success. We give kudos to people who have succeeded. We don't care in what they succeeded as long as they succeeded. The worst thing that can happen to anybody in this cultural environment is to fail.

Desmond Tutu in an interview with U. Mertens, from *THE FOCUS*, and John J. Grumbar, from Egon Zehnder (2017)

At the start of the COVID pandemic, when all our church buildings were closed, services suddenly had to go online. Some churches live-streamed their services on platforms such as YouTube or Facebook Live. Others presented pre-recorded offerings. Almost overnight, we all became experts in video editing. Up and down the country, in ministry home studies and vicarage gardens everywhere, clergy families were roped into producing this week's service, sermon, prayers and songs. All it took was a decent phone and some basic video-editing software and you too could create offerings as professional as the BBC. Well, nearly. It took a while to get the hang of it and it was infuriating when you got almost to the end of your beautifully

19

crafted sermon, stumbled over your words and had to start all over again.

Gradually, I noticed a few of these 'bloopers' appearing in the timelines of friends' social media pages. One day I thought it might be fun to gather a few together and make something of them. So I put out an appeal on Facebook for people to send in clips of themselves doing silly things and making mistakes in the process of putting together online worship. I was inundated. There were kids joining in loudly at key moments of prayer, dogs wandering around in the background during sermons, muddled words, lots of corpsing, one person's prayer interrupted almost completely by crows. I spliced all the clips together with some silly music in the background and put a message of thanks to everyone for their efforts at the end, including a deliberate spelling mistake for good measure. The resulting video was more widely shared and 'liked' than anything I've ever put out there before or since. Why? What was its appeal?

I think it was popular because everyone recognized themselves in it. We had all been trying so hard, sending out and posting the polished final, edited versions, but when people saw others failing as they had been in the making of them, it was a great encouragement. Plus it was very funny.

There is something intrinsically compelling and endearing about watching failures or mistakes or cock-ups, so long as no one gets hurt. The Mischief Theatre has made a huge success out of the 'Goes Wrong' series of plays and programmes: *The Play that Goes Wrong*, *Peter Pan Goes Wrong*, *Magic Goes Wrong*. All of them portray familiar dramatic themes and contexts, but with a series of deliberate mistakes that become increasingly more dramatic and hilarious – lines missed, props mislaid, scenery toppling. As it says on the company's website:

> We believe that everyone should have the opportunity to break free from the shackles of everyday life and escape with us to a world of carefully choreographed chaos, merry mishaps and timeless comedy. A place where you can escape reality and laugh until you cry.[1]

Failure can be hilarious and we love it.

We also hate failure. No sooner does a person do or say something considered to be wrong by others, or is found to have said the wrong thing once many years ago when they were very young, than they are immediately cast by popular opinion into outer darkness, where there is wailing and gnashing of teeth. Mostly on Twitter.

So why do we love and cherish some failure, finding it entertaining, and decry and refuse to tolerate other kinds of failure? What's the difference, and where is the dividing line to be drawn between what is acceptable and funny and what is abhorrent, offensive and dangerous?

We will return to this question shortly but, first, we need to make sure that we are talking about the same thing. What do we mean by 'failure' and what is it anyway?

What is failure?

The word 'failure' comes from the Old French verb *faillir*, meaning 'to lack' or 'to fail', derived from the Latin verb *fallere.* Old French also had the corresponding nouns *faille*, *faillance*, *faillement* and *faleur*, all meaning 'lack' or 'fault'. In English, however, the word was originally a verb only – 'to fail' – and it was not until the seventeenth century that the '-ure' ending was added to make it a noun. Even then, it only began to be applied to people – 'a failure' – in 1837. I don't know what happened in 1837 that caused someone to be called, for the first time, 'a failure'. Must have been awful. It's the year Queen Victoria came to the throne, so maybe that had something to do with it.

There's a certain atmosphere attached to the word. When I was writing this book, I had some discussion with the publishers about its title. The conversation went a bit like this.

'What's the book about?'

'Failure.'

'Ah. We're not sure anyone will buy a book with the title *Failure*. [That may still be true.] Shall we try something else? Maybe something a bit more cheerful?'

'But it's about failure.'

'Ah, OK. How about "Fail*ing*", then? Does that sound better?'

'No.'

I can see their point. No one likes to be thought of as a failure, and I can also see that this might be a tricky book to buy to give to someone else, but the fact is that failure is part of all our lives and there's no getting away from it.

Maybe you *can* buy a book entitled *Failure* without implicating yourself too much, since it remains abstract. 'Failures' may be OK also. Making it plural, to my mind, softens the blow somewhat. That implies a series of things going wrong, not just one large one. I fail, you fail, we all fail. Maybe 'fail*ing*' *is* better. It implies an active involvement with failure – an ongoing failure – that somehow seems more comfortable and, probably, is more accurate.

The trouble with 'failing', though, is that it's also the adjective we attach to things – institutions, often – that are not doing very well at all. OFSTED categorizes a school as a 'failing' school; a church may be discussed at a bishop's leadership team meeting as a 'failing church'. The tenor of this epithet is that the thing in question requires improvement and, hopefully, steps are taken to help set that in train, but it never feels good to be labelled 'failing'.

Worst of all is 'a failure'. It is a name. A title. An identity. Not just someone who fails or deals with failure but is, inside and out, A Failure. End of. It feels so final. There's not much coming back from that. As psychotherapist and author Colin Feltham says, however, 'it seems unlikely, if not impossible, for anyone actually to *be* a (total) failure . . . Any of us may fail at certain things but none of us can be a perfect failure'.[2] So perhaps when we speak about failure, or failing, we should take pains to watch our language and use terms to express the fact that we've all fallen short, and most of us fail every single day, but none of us is beyond redemption. None of us is – interminably – A Failure.

This book is about failure but, of course, the word is a blanket term for all sorts of ways in which things might go wrong. What is the difference, for instance, between failures and mistakes, faults and errors? John C. Maxwell writes:

> Every person's life is filled with errors and negative experiences. But know this: Errors become mistakes when we perceive them and respond to them incorrectly. Mistakes become failures when we continually respond to them incorrectly. People who fail forward are able to see errors or negative experiences as a regular part of life, learn from them and then move on.[3]

Mistakes, then, are to be seen as a kind of failure in which learning can happen and are, therefore, not to be shied away from, so long as they are the kinds of mistakes that do not lead to catastrophic failure. One study suggests that making mistakes is, in fact, necessary to rewire the brain, creating new synapses that lead to increased learning.[4]

The problem comes when mistakes are made constantly and consecutively, but neither acknowledged nor learnt from. Merope Mills tells the heart-rending story of the death of her daughter Martha following a cycling accident. A series of mistakes made in the hospital during her care were not recognized, rectified and learnt from, mainly due to a culture of deference towards, and inability to challenge the views of, senior medics. She writes about how one doctor 'was very reluctant to use the word "mistake" to describe his actions, though his error had been identified by colleagues'.[5] Some mistakes can be fatal, and we need

24

to do all we can to prevent those happening or happening again.

Failures, mistakes and errors occur in every area of work and in every walk of life. Much of the writing about and study of failure has been done in connection with industries in which such errors have the potential to lead to great harm to people, such as the construction industry. The UK Health and Safety Executive, for example, names two types of failure: 'human error' ('an unintentional action or decision') and 'violations' ('deliberately doing the wrong thing'), either due to lack of choice or lack of concern about the consequences. Human error is divided into three categories: 'slips' ('Not doing what you're meant to do'), 'lapses' ('Forgetting to do something, or losing your place midway through a task') and 'mistakes' ('decision-making failures'). Mistakes can be either rule-based or knowledge-based and 'arise when we do the wrong thing, believing it to be right'.[6]

One study defines a 'mistake' as 'a deviation from a norm or a standard' and an 'error' as 'a wrong assumption, idea or behaviours'. 'Failure' is defined as 'a lack of success in desired goals or values due to complex situations and circumstances.[7] But this leads us to the questions 'Who specifies the goals that are not met?' and 'Who decides what these are?'

In defining something as a failure, there must be an agreed standard that has not been reached and, often, there isn't one or there is no agreement about what the standard is, which is where the problems start. Elizabeth Day, interviewer on her hugely popular podcast, 'How to fail with Elizabeth Day', defines failure simply as 'what happens when something doesn't go according to plan'.[8] But this again leads us to the question 'Whose plan is it anyway?'

In order to know whether something is a failure you need to know which plan it didn't go according to. And sometimes we are considered to have failed due to other peoples' expectations being wrong. Jesus looked like a failure if you class success as having lots of followers and building his own empire, and not being crucified before the age of 33. But according to God's plan – the redemption of humanity and eternal salvation through death and resurrection – he was a resounding success.

All books on failure start with a definition of the word 'failure', but even that is not straightforward. The standard dictionary definition – 'lack of success in doing or achieving something'[9] – doesn't really begin to capture the nuance and cadence of what failure is or feels like. It's easy to define failure in terms of facts: it is 'the fact of someone or something not succeeding',[10] but we know instinctively, because we are human, that it is far more than that and such definitions really pose more questions than they answer about what failure actually is.

Feltham describes the problem associated with defining failure and says, 'Obviously it refers to some sort of breakdown, some malfunctioning or underperformance',[11] but then goes on to question whether perfect performance – the myth that 'things should always function without fail' – is ever a possibility anyway. Failure is not simply the opposite of success. It is not a mere short-lived inconvenience through which we pass on the way to getting it all right all the time. In many ways it is our natural state of being.

Russ Parker writes in the preface to his book on failure that 'failure will always be one of the ingredients of life that will be the hardest to live with and yet yield some of the greatest opportunities to become truly real.'[12]

When I have told people that I am writing a book on failure, and how successful it will be (joke), invariably there passes across each of their faces a look of recognition, an acknowledgement, a sense of 'Ah, yes, we've all been there', a shared experience. Lots of people said to me, with a wry chuckle, 'Oh, I've got plenty of examples, should you need any.' Liverpool academic Joe Moran, in his wonderfully encouraging small book *If You Should Fail*, speaks of failure in these terms: 'Failure is not a holding station we pass through on the way to somewhere else. It is its own country, where we must all learn to live.' We are all permanent citizens of the Republic of Failure. 'Failure', he says, 'is home.'[13]

Perhaps this is the start of understanding what failure is and what role it plays in the lives of people, and of Christians in particular. Maybe we need to stop shying away from failure in embarrassment and shame, and learn to embrace it. If not a welcome presence in our lives, at least we can come to accept that it's always likely to be there, so we need to learn to live with it.

Negligence, weakness and our own deliberate fault: a typology of failures

All failures are not equal. We tend to lump them all together, but there are differences. Is a genuine mistake the same as a devious moral error? How do we tell the difference? We need a way to categorize failures to help us understand what we might embrace, even encourage and learn from, and what we might wish to avoid at all costs.

Amy Edmondson's contention is that some failures are to be encouraged, while others are to be avoided. Some warrant praise and are the gateway to new breakthroughs. Others warrant blame and demand admission, an apology and reparation. The trouble is, we're not very good at telling the difference between them.

She suggests that there are three primary kinds of failure.[14] First, there are simple, preventable failures or mistakes made in routine tasks. The person knows how to do something right but, for some reason, gets it wrong. She says, 'They usually involve deviations from spec in the closely defined processes of high-volume or routine operations in manufacturing and services.'[15] These are simple mistakes in processes that involve human error. Someone knew what to do but forgot or neglected to do it properly.

Second, there are complex failures or accidents, which is when a set of factors *together* lead to failure, despite there being recognized processes. A report into the fatal train crash at Stonehaven in 2020, in which three people died, states that the train derailed because it struck debris that had washed out of a badly constructed drainage trench during a period of heavy rain, which had placed the controllers, who had not been given guidance or training to enable them to manage such complex situations, under 'severe workload pressure' due to the volume of weather-related events. Additionally, the train in question was an

older model that didn't include design features to minimize damage in a collision. The train crash was the result
of a complex failure.

Finally, there are intelligent failures – that is, discoveries
which are the undesired results of 'thoughtful forays into
new territory'. When Thomas Edison was asked about the
failures he experienced on the way to inventing the electric
lightbulb, he said (purportedly), 'I have not failed 10,000
times – I've successfully found 10,000 ways that will not
work'. Intelligent failures should be looked for and embraced.

Edmondson holds that – particularly in contexts where
'we haven't been there before', pioneering situations,
uncertain times, in which answers are not knowable in
advance – risk taking (with the attendant potential for
failure) is absolutely essential:

> At the frontier, the right kind of experimentation
> produces good failures quickly. Managers who practice
> [sic] it can avoid the unintelligent failure of conducting
> experiments at a larger scale than necessary.[16]

The knack with intelligent failure is to make sure that
you're taking risks in the areas that really matter for your
organization's mission and purpose. The key to failing
really intelligently is first to identify what success looks
like in your context – that is, what your organization is for,
and therefore what risks it can afford to take. A laboratory
can explore risk taking and possible failure as part of its
raison d'être. A surgical team or a nuclear plant probably
shouldn't. What really matters is defining your purpose,

knowing how you would recognize success and, therefore, knowing where you can safely risk failure.

Edmondson has also identified a spectrum of reasons for why failures happen.[17] The spectrum ranges from reasons that are blameworthy at '1' to praiseworthy at '9', as follows:

1 **deviance** an individual chooses to violate a prescribed process or practice;
2 **inattention** an individual inadvertently deviates from the specifications;
3 **lack of ability** an individual doesn't have the skills, conditions or training to execute a job;
4 **process inadequacy** a competent individual adheres to a prescribed but faulty or incomplete process;
5 **task challenge** an individual faces a task too difficult to be executed reliably every time;
6 **process complexity** a process composed of many elements breaks down when it encounters novel interactions;
7 **uncertainty** a lack of clarity about future events causes people to take seemingly reasonable actions that produce undesired results;
8 **hypothesis testing** an experiment conducted to prove that an idea or a design will succeed fails;
9 **exploratory testing** an experiment conducted to expand knowledge and investigate a possibility leads to an undesired result.

Edmondson contends that very few failures are someone's deliberate fault and, in many organizations, blame is apportioned more frequently than it should be. She says that when it comes to evaluating whether a failure is considered blameworthy or praiseworthy, we tend to overplay external factors that led to our *own* mistakes, but underplay them when it comes to the mistakes of others. We let ourselves off the hook too readily and fail to afford the same courtesy to others:

> We . . . tend to downplay our responsibility and place undue blame on external or situational factors when we fail, only to do the reverse when assessing the failures of others – a psychological trap known as fundamental attribution error.[18]

The result when more is considered blameworthy than needs be is that fear abounds and people are afraid of taking even potentially constructive risks for fear of getting it wrong and being blamed, with serious consequences. Such fear gets in the way of the opportunity for learning described above.

Edmondson suggests that failure analysis needs to move beyond the simple ('Who did what wrong?') and on to the complex ('Why and what systems and structures led to their mistake?'). It is the contention of this book that failure is here to stay and simply seeing it as something to get over or avoid to achieve success is to misunderstand the power and potential – and the reality – of failure. Yet surely it is better to learn from failure than not? This is not easy. When we are confronted with things that have gone wrong, we can feel embarrassment and shame, try to cover up the results and hope the whole situation will go away. Or we can look it full in the face to find out what happened and learn to do things differently next time. What prevents this kind of learning from happening as often as it should?

The fear factor

The primary thing that stops organizations, and the people within them, making the kinds of failures that may lead to success is fear, fear of getting it wrong. Such fear takes several forms: fear that we will be found inadequate for the task, fear of harming ourselves or other people (though that is probably a good fear to have), fear that we will be embarrassed or shamed.

A degree of fear of failure is to be welcomed. It is that kind of healthy fear which is the precursor to trying new things. It shows we are moving into areas that we have not been in before and are not sure how things will turn out. But some fear of failure is altogether less positive and even crippling. There is a word for an extreme fear of failure: 'atychiphobia', which is an abnormal, unwarranted and persistent fear of failing at something in your life.

At the root of our fear of failure is a fear of shame, 'the intensely painful feeling or experience of believing that we are flawed and therefore unworthy of love, belonging, and connection'.[19] There is an embarrassment connected with failure. When we fail, we feel that we are incompetent, not up to the job, somehow less. Moran puts it like this: 'Shame still attaches to failure as it ever has. That is why we are so quick to turn it into something else, to escape from its shame with stories of salvation.'[20]

Brené Brown, who has written extensively on the topic of vulnerability and shame in the context of leadership suggests that there are several possible reactions to the experience of shame: to move away from it and withdraw, becoming silent and keeping secrets, to move towards other people, seeking to appease and please, or to move against the shame, by being aggressive and trying to gain power over others. All those reactions have implications for the way in which failure is seen and responded to and all diminish the people who have acted in such ways. Brown speaks of reacting differently and of the benefits of being 'wholehearted' people, 'those people who live from a deep sense of worthiness, who possess a deep sense of courage. They have the courage to be imperfect. They treat themselves with kindness and are able to show kindness to others. In the words of Jesus, they are capable of loving their neighbours as themselves'.[21]

So why does failure happen and why are we so keen to cover it up when it does? In their book *Mistakes Were Made (but Not by Me)*, Carol Tavris and Elliott Aronson examine the concept of 'cognitive dissonance' (a term coined by psychologist Leon Festinger in the middle of the twentieth century). Tavris and Aronson define cognitive dissonance as 'a state of tension that occurs when a person holds two cognitions (ideas, attitudes, beliefs, opinions) that are psychologically inconsistent with each other'.[22] Such discomfort when there is dissonance springs from the inner need of human beings to create a narrative that enables us to lead a life that is 'consistent and meaningful'. The trouble is, things go wrong and we don't know why or what to do about it. We justify ourselves and our world to make sense of what we see and experience every day. In connection with failure, cognitive dissonance drives the impulse to downplay, deny or cover up failure. Humans go to great lengths to avoid the pain and shame that goes with failure and so will employ all kinds of tactics to ensure that it doesn't happen, either denying or minimizing it. That is what causes people to prefer to tell a fabricated story about what went wrong and why, even when confronted with the facts, to avoid the pain and shame of confessing they got it wrong, even to themselves. It is this self-justification that causes people to veer away from openly admitting mistakes. The root of it all is the self-protection necessary for the avoidance of shame.

The first step towards learning from failure, therefore, is to get things out into the open. For that to happen, the shame and stigma of failure must be recognized. Many failures are not picked up because there is a fear of talking about them. Edmondson contends that it is up to leaders of organizations (who she calls the 'higher-ups') to create the kind of culture in which shame does not pervade and open admission of failure leads to learning for all:

When failure is detected, failure analysis needs to be carried out enthusiastically and with courage in order for learning to occur. But various factors including shame, embarrassment, 'loyalty' to colleagues, and a host of other things get in the way of that happening as often as it should.[23]

Tavris and Aronson, likewise, suggest that 'institutions can be designed to reward admissions of mistakes as part of the organizational culture rather than making it uncomfortable or professionally risky for people to come forward. This design, naturally, must come from the top.'[24]

Fear of failure in a social media age

Accepting that the fear of shame associated with failure can stifle the kind of risk-taking, failure and rediscovery that leads to innovation is the first step when creating a learning culture. And that leads us to redefine failure. Matthew Syed, in his book *Black Box Thinking*, which examines a series of failures leading to creative breakthroughs, cites several organizations who have embraced 'failure parties' or similar to destigmatize failure. He cites a school that has initiated a 'failure week' and quotes the headteacher of that school:

You're not born with fear of failure, it's not an instinct, it's something that grows and develops in you as you get older. Very young children have no fear of failure at all. They have great fun trying new things and learning very fast. Our focus here is on failing well, on being good at failure. What I mean by this is taking the risk and then learning from it if it doesn't work.

Once you've identified the learning you can then take action to make a difference.[25]

Syed therefore advocates a redefining of failure along the following lines:

When you regard failure as a learning opportunity, when you trust in the power of practice to help you grow through difficulties, your motivation and self-belief are not threatened in anything like the same way. Indeed, you embrace failure as an opportunity to learn, whether about improving a vacuum cleaner, creating a new scientific theory, or developing a promising football career.[26]

We need to be able to fail in order to risk and innovate, and in uncertain times that is even more the case. People are angry, disillusioned and disorientated, they are calling out for certainty. The parlous state of our nations and economies means that we are unsure who will get us out of this mess and are calling out for someone to do something. We are simultaneously suspicious of authority and angry with institutions, yet calling for the grown-ups to sort out the mess for us. Only there aren't any grown-ups any more. As soon as something goes wrong, therefore, the cry goes up, 'Who did this? Who is to blame? Who must pay the price?'

I experienced something of this when I was involved with organizing a conference. A very big conference, involving thousands of people from around the world. In the run-up to the conference (which went very well in the end), a change was made in the presentation of some of the documents associated with the event. It wasn't a mistake made by any one person. It was a series of well-intentioned interventions by several parties that, ultimately, had a damaging impact and led to an understandable outcry.

I was not directly involved in the processes that led to the bad outcome, but I failed to pick up on it, and was seen to defend something that was later found to be problematic for a variety of reasons. Did I make the fateful changes myself? No. Did I fail? Yes. I didn't check communications carefully enough. I didn't check the work of others and trusted too readily that procedures were being followed properly. I didn't communicate with colleagues clearly enough. I allowed myself to get too busy so I didn't deal with some basic tasks well. I did a press conference that I was ill-prepared for. Probably other things in addition.

How could I admit my own inevitable failure with respect to the events without implicating others in the process? That's difficult. Let me say it clearly now: I'm sorry. Am I sorry that my failure had an impact on the lives of people and potentially damaged the goodwill of many towards the conference and, ultimately, the Church I work within? Very much so. Did I act alone? No. Was it all 'my fault'? Not really. Would I do things differently next time? You bet.

I learnt several things. Failure, particularly as a leader, is complex and multilayered. And, as very few mistakes are entirely one person's fault, owning up and saying sorry are complex matters too. Oh, and check your communications more carefully. And speak up when you think something's not right.

As Edmondson has shown, few failures have a simple cause. More usually, they are a complex series of events – some of them personal, some organizational, some circumstantial – that lead to something going wrong or not as well as it should have done. Things are sometimes, but probably rarely, one person's fault.

Resignations may make the mob feel better but they don't always get to the heart of the problem or enable effective learning to happen. To admit failure, there must be a space in which people can do so without feeling fearful of the consequences. They must feel that their admissions will be treated with fairness and justice, certainly, but also with reason and kindness. And sometimes they must be given the opportunity to try again.

Some kinds of failure really hurt and damage other people and the leadership needs to take responsibility, apologies need to be made, lessons learned, reparative action taken. The trouble is that failure is rarely as simple, the solutions as straightforward, as @angryperson would like to believe: 'We have to atone, we have to take responsibility, we have to despise what we have done and we have to apologise to those we have hurt. But we do not, in the end, have to be without kindness for ourselves.'[27]

As we've seen, despite our confusion about what to do when it happens in real life, failure is trendy. You're supposed to fail, we're told. It's inevitable. The important thing is that you pick yourself up, learn lessons and move on. Failure is the pathway to greater success: 'Ever tried. Ever failed. No matter. Try again. Fail again. Fail better.' The problem with the 'It's OK to fail and just pick yourself up and try again' mantra is that we do not live in an age where such failure is easily permissible. Not if you're a leader who lives life in the public gaze anyway. The problem with the 'Fail Often. Fail Well' mantra is that it doesn't factor in someone demanding to know who got it wrong and what is to be done about it, baying for your head on a block at every turn. The problem with the encouragement to fail and learn from it is that it assumes a fairly level context, a predictable set of circumstances in which the failure happens, a clear location of wrongdoing, a secure set of institutions able to respond systematically, putting things right for the next time, a level-headed and understanding public willing to receive the apology and allow trying again, a modicum of grace that says, 'It's OK. We've all been there. Go on. Have another go.' None of that is terribly evident in the world, nor even in the Church, today.

The 'Ever tried. Ever failed' quotation above is from Samuel Beckett, the Irish playwright whose works were grouped with those of others who had a pessimistic view of the human condition and termed the 'Theatre of the Absurd'. Not the most obvious candidate for an inspirational quotation of the kind to appear on T-shirts and reusable tote bags. The wider context of the quotation reveals the hopeless, nihilistic context in which his words appear. Far from being a perky truism aimed at inspiring budding entrepreneurs, it is, rather, a desperate and depressing admission in a volley of fractured and increasingly nonsensical utterances:

> Ever tried. Ever failed. No matter. Try again. Fail again. Fail better. First the body. No. First the place. No. First both. Now either. Now the other. Sick of the either try the other. Sick of it back sick of the either. So on. Somehow on. Till sick of both. Throw up and go. Where neither. Till sick of there. Throw up and back. The body again. Where none. The place again. Where none. Try again. Fail again. Better again. Or better worse. Fail worse again. Still worse again. Till sick for good. Throw up for good. Go for good. Where neither for good. Good and all.[28]

What do we do about that? What do you do when 'Fail worse again' much more accurately sums up your experience than 'Fail better'? What kind of leadership during failure is required and survivable in these fevered, fractious times?

One of the greatest issues for our world, our Church and anyone in leadership of either at present is anxiety. Anxiety is a modern disease and perpetual state of mind. As I write, on this particular day, the UK is still reeling from the effects of the COVID pandemic (and I have tested positive myself). The war in Ukraine that has shaken Europe so profoundly continues to have an impact on the cost of goods, from fuel to bread. The UK has experienced its hottest temperatures on record as the effects of the climate catastrophe known so well throughout the rest of the world, especially developing countries, finally makes its presence felt in our bodies and on our surroundings in the West. Fires are rife, even in the usually green and lush suburbs. Yesterday evening, I watched video footage of a house burning to the ground in west London as a result of a wildfire. The cost of energy has soared and the UK government is in talks with the energy companies to see if anything can be done about the impending predicted £5,000 per year energy bill that lies in wait for the average household this autumn and winter. Years of underinvestment have had drastic impacts on our health and education systems. There are hundreds of thousands of people waiting for surgery. The rail workers have just announced another tranche of strikes in protest over pay and conditions. And that is just a snapshot of what is in the news today. No wonder we feel anxious. Even I, writing from the perspective of a reasonably well-resourced, middle-aged, healthy, middle-class person with a secure income, feel anxious. I can't begin to imagine how all this feels if you are on the breadline or unable to work or disabled. Or young. The young people of my children's generation tell me that they fear what the future will hold.

Mark Sayer writes about non-anxious leadership in an anxious world and posits that:

In our day, anxiety has become one of the significant ailments of our world. Yet it is also a signal, an alarm that something is desperately wrong in our world. We must differentiate between the individual mental health challenge of anxiety, which a minority of individuals experience, and the systemic anxiety that our contemporary culture's structures create.[29]

We do indeed live in anxious times. The failure of nearly everything seems very real. 'Breaking news' used to be read or listened to with interest; now it's with terror: what on earth has happened now?

Living in complex, unpredictable times demands certain characteristics if we are to navigate it successfully. One of the prime traits we need is acceptance that complexity is the order of the day, there are no simple solutions and to be honest about that. One of the failures of the UK government during the pandemic, asserts businesswoman and writer Margaret Heffernan, was that they too often peddled certainty and predictable outcomes where there were none – 'over by Christmas', 'follow the science', 'return to normal' – when what was actually needed was the creation of a shared narrative of reality and the honest admission that ambiguity and uncertainty were likely to continue for some time. People are not stupid. We knew that there had been failure – we saw and experienced it all around us during the pandemic, in the closed churches, overwhelmed emergency services, the preparation of overflow hospitals, small weddings, Christmas alone. What we needed then, and need now, from our institutions and leaders is the frank admission that *no one* can predict accurately what the future holds, no one can be completely confident what the best solutions are and failure is something we all need to learn to live with, not cover up with platitudes and slogans.

Sorry. Rant over.

Christians and failure

Christians ought to be really good at failure. The story of our faith equips us so well for it. I often say this, but if I'd been writing the Bible, I would have gone about it differently. I would have been tempted to big up the highlights and play down the bad bits, to show the story of God's people in an altogether more positive light. But the *real* sorry story of God's people contained in the Bible and written in the books of all our lives from here to eternity is one of constant failure. Redemption also, of course, and grace and love and all those other good things, but all those good things are necessary because the people of God fail and always have done. We'll look at this further in later chapters, but for now we note that, although @Anglican_Twitter can, at times, seem the least forgiving of places, Christians ought to be the ones most familiar with, and accepting of, failure. We should also be the most forgiving when it comes to those who fail. Is there room in our theology for a doctrine of failure?

Jesus set out very clearly to his disciples and in several places that what they were signing up to was not an instant route to worldly success. It wasn't going to earn them a good reputation or honour or glory. It would, in all likelihood, lead to their deaths: 'If any want to become my followers, let them deny themselves and take up their cross and follow me' (Matthew 16.24). Even with large crowds following him, Jesus clearly spelt out the cost of discipleship and that it is not an easy ask: 'Whoever comes to me and does not hate father and mother, wife and children, brothers and sisters, yes, and even life itself, cannot be my disciple' (Luke 14.26).

When Jesus' disciples were arguing over which of them was the most successful and would sit in the most honoured place in heaven, Jesus was clear that's not what all this is about: 'But it is not so among you; instead whoever wishes to become great among you must be your servant, and whoever wishes to be first among you must be slave of all' (Mark 10.43–44). It's why Dietrich Bonhoeffer summed up discipleship in this way: 'When Christ calls a man he bids him come and die.'[30] Jesus knew that to be a follower of his would not be an easy path to walk, and he prepared his followers well for failure.

As we've seen, one of the things that we fear when admitting failure is the spectre of shame. The reason so many people don't admit to mistakes and errors is that we don't acknowledge the inevitability of failure as part of the human condition and we think that if we admit to getting something wrong, we'll be seen as incompetent. One day people will realize that I am the fraud I know myself to be, as the self-talk goes.

I reckon that, for most people – aside from those rare few who seem somehow to have an unfailing sense of confidence in their own ability – most of the time, adult life is lived in constant fear of being found out. 'Imposter syndrome' looms large. Grown-up life is hard work. It involves constant making of decisions and daily actions that, if done wrongly, potentially, could end in disaster. Indeed, some of us have a very highly tuned sense of the perilousness of adult life. I think it's why I hate driving. I don't trust myself and I'm so conscious of all the terrible things that could result if I make a wrong move. I'd be a terrible pilot.

In some ways, we need to maintain the veneer of competence. It wouldn't do if, each time I went to the dentist, she started with the words, 'I hope this goes OK. I really don't know what I'm doing,' or the train driver chirpily let you know over the tannoy, 'I'm 80 per cent confident that I'll get you to your destination relatively unscathed.' Keeping up the aura of respectability and competence ensures that we function as people and societies. Yet, there is always the nagging fear just below the surface that I'll be found out. That's why it is wonderful, even in this place of fear, that the Christian story speaks loud and clear. We fear shame, yet at the heart of the story of Christ is the comforting fact that the Son of God, who was in all senses the most perfect human who has ever lived, sinless and whole in a way none of the rest of us will ever be, was himself the subject of shame, mockery and derision. At the heart of the good news of Jesus Christ stands a symbol of foolishness and utter incompetence – the cross.

We often miss what a shameful failure the cross appeared to be. We have cast it now in the warm glow of the success of the resurrection and perhaps are inclined to skip over what a sign of ignominy the crucifixion of Christ really was at that time. After his trial, the soldiers guarding him clothed him with ironic symbols of success precisely to highlight how much he had failed in the eyes of those who condemned him to death: 'They stripped him and put a scarlet robe on him, and after twisting some thorns into a crown, they put it on his head. They put a reed in his right hand. and knelt before him and mocked him, saying, "Hail, King of the Jews!"' (Matthew 27.28–29). He couldn't even carry his own cross. As Jesus was crucified, those looking on held out to him what they thought he had said about his own success and goaded him with his failure: 'You who would destroy the temple and build it in three days, save yourself! If you are the Son of God, come down from the cross' (Matthew 27.40). The religious leaders also mocked him, saying, 'He saved others; he cannot save himself' (Matthew 27.42). Failure.

Even though Jesus was the perfect human being who could never sin and could not fail in the eyes of God, he certainly *seemed* to be a failure in the eyes of the world. Right at the heart of the Christian faith stands a symbol of shame and disgrace. It was widely held that execution by crucifixion was not only cruel but also humiliating. Yet it is through the cross, a powerful icon of failure, that God chose to shame the apparent wisdom of this world:

> Much of the power of Christianity derives from the wisdom of the cross regarding suffering, failure and death. It is a realistic preparation for the inevitable experience of personal and social failure: 'you will be hated by all men on account of my name' (Matthew 10.22).[31]

Perhaps another word for the shame of failure is 'foolishness'. When we fail, we feel foolish, and the Bible has plenty to say about that too: 'But God chose what is foolish in the world to shame the wise; God chose what is weak in the world to shame the strong' (1 Corinthians 1.27). Paul makes the bold claim that through this shameful instrument of public humiliation God showed his ultimate wisdom and power. That ought to offer comfort to all of us who feel like we have failed. Failure is never final and redemption is always possible.

So what's the problem? Why are we, even those of us who are Christians, so reluctant to allow ourselves and others to fail? Why do we have such an undeveloped theology of failure? Without a robust theology of failure, we are unable truly to know ourselves or to know the extent of God's love, grace and forgiveness. As John Navone says:

> Such a theology must remind us that there is no authentic Christianity without the willingness to risk failure and that to attempt to insulate ourselves from the possibility of failure is a betrayal of the Christian spirit, so that our attitude toward failure measures the degree of our self-transcendence in Christ.[32]

Part of the problem, I believe, is that we don't allow ourselves to have very good role models.

Imperfect saints

Every morning, in the chapel at Lambeth Palace where I live (in a humble cottage in the grounds, I hasten to add, not in the palace itself), the community of people who live here say morning prayer together. It's a community of around 35, including the Archbishop of Canterbury and his family, members of the Community of St Anselm (young people who come to take 'a year in God's time' to develop and grow their relationship with God and God's world) and some nuns. There are usually also staff members who work at Lambeth Palace who wish to begin their day with quiet prayer.

Every day the same simple pattern of prayer is followed and most days we start by reading from a book called *Exciting Holiness*,[33] which is about the saint whom we remember that day. Coming from a fairly Low Church tradition myself, this has been a revelation. I would be lying if I were to tell you that it has awakened in me a deep desire to delve further into hagiography, but I love it because the lives of these saints are so fascinating. I recall several as being of particular note. There's Brigid of Kildare (1 February), known for her prayers and miracles, also said to have been consecrated the first female bishop, mainly because she apparently bore a strong physical resemblance to the Virgin Mary. There's Denys, Bishop of Paris (9 October), who planted a church and is said to have continued preaching even after his head was cut off. Those are among the stranger ones.

Day by day we hear the stories of these great women and men of faith, who are much to be admired. I have to confess, however, I spend most of the time thinking that I could never ever live up to their examples of holiness and devotion. My book of saints would be called *Rather Dull and Ordinary Holiness* and would be a set of realistic stories of the saints. Every saint's day listing would have an example of one thing that they got really badly wrong to encourage all us mere mortals: 'This is Perpetua – she got eaten by lions and was really holy and all that, but she was also really grumpy and a bit of a drama queen, to be honest.' That would be far more inspiring – and encouraging for the likes of the rest of us.

How many buildings have had to be renamed, statues removed, paintings taken down, monuments repositioned when the people we thought we admired and named things after were found to be heinous sinners and guilty of all manner of crimes and misdemeanours? How many incidents of harm might have been avoided if the perpetrator had not been thought to be wholly good and, therefore, not possibly capable of what they were being accused of – too famous, too eminent, too wonderful?

The trouble with putting people on pedestals (sometimes literally) is that they are liable to fall off . . . or be dragged off. Perhaps we need to recalibrate our assessments of both saints and sinners, for Christians are always both at the same time. We could do ourselves and those around us a great favour if we owned up to the failures we really are and admired people not because they are very good or very holy, but because they are people whom God loves, warts and all.

The Archbishop of Canterbury tells a story of going to a church where he was preaching about the subject of sin. During his sermon, he made the point that all have sinned and fallen short of the glory of God, including himself. After the service he was approached by an outraged woman who exclaimed in disgust, 'Archbishop! I did not know that you were a sinner!', adding, before harrumphing away, her illusions about the Primate of All England in tatters, 'If I had known you were a sinner, I would not have come today!'

Simply unfinished

We started this chapter with a definition of failure as simply what happens 'when something doesn't go to plan'. Again, we return to the question, 'Whose plan?' If the plan is the plan of the world, the flesh and the devil, then Jesus failed, we fail, the Church is an abject failure. But if the plan is God's blueprint for a new way of living, a new way of being, a different and alternative vision of what constitutes success, then the landscape looks different.

The only plan that counts is the vision for kingdom living inaugurated by Jesus, announced at the beginning of his ministry (Matthew 3.2; Mark 1.15), entrusted to his disciples and which continues through his Church today. That plan completely redraws the map of what constitutes success and failure. According to the ways of the kingdom of God, you are successful not when you are rich and famous and when everything is going swimmingly. You succeed when you look like you're failing, when you give yourself for others, when you pay most attention to the least, the lost, the last, when you seek first the kingdom.

The kingdom of heaven is like this: a widow looking for a lost coin, buried treasure, a dying grain of wheat. The first shall be last. As Christians, we ought not to seek perfection and success this side of heaven, for we will be continually disappointed. We ought instead relentlessly to pursue God's kingdom above all else, living with the uncertainty and mess that is this present age, as we await the fulfilment of the children of God, all of us failures.

Most of life is lived feeling as though there is no plan at all. What if even God doesn't have the perfect plan? But there is, and he does. We live in anxious times and certainty is impossible to come by. Of course, God knows everything and knows what will happen when, but he spares us the anxiety of being in on all that, of knowing too much too soon. That should free us to live each failure-laden day at a time without striving to calculate whether we've lived up to the standards – ours or anyone else's. We're not finished, but we're on the way.

The African American poet Amanda Gorman, in her wonderful poem read at the inauguration of the President of the USA, Joe Biden, 'The hill we climb', spoke of being not 'broken' but 'simply unfinished'.[34]

What if we're all not broken, not failures, but simply unfinished?

For discussion

1 Think of an example of failure that you love and another that you hate. What was the difference between them?
2 How does fear of failure affect your ability to learn from your mistakes?
3 How do you deal with the anxiety and uncertainty that contemporary culture causes?

3

Sin, guilt and human nature: towards an imperfect theology of failure (sort of)

> Be a sinner, and let your sins be strong, but let your trust in Christ be stronger, and rejoice in Christ who is the victor over sin, death, and the world . . . Pray hard for you are quite a sinner.
>
> Martin Luther, A Letter from Luther to Melanchthon (Letter no. 99, 1 August 1521)

I have long held that one of the most comforting doctrines of the Christian faith is the doctrine of total depravity. How so? Well, it seems to me that when things are as low as they can go, then they can go no lower. When we're thinking about what it means to fail, that's quite a comforting thought. We start from a low point and work up, rather than start with idolization and wait for people to fall off their pedestals.

The doctrine of total depravity is the belief, expressed by John Calvin, that human beings are completely sinful. By that he means every part of the human condition is affected by the sinfulness that entered the world and its people when Adam and Eve first ate the forbidden fruit in Eden:

Original sin, then, may be defined as hereditary corruption and depravity of our nature, extending to all the parts of the soul, which first makes us obnoxious to the wrath of God, and then produces in us works which in Scripture are termed works of the flesh.[1]

Even writers and thinkers who express no Christian or any other kind of religious belief point to the fact that all is not as it should be with the human race. Psychology professor Colin Feltham, for example, admits that:

we human beings have a serious, chronic, unaddressed failure at our core. We may balk at calling it original sin or a species flaw, but there is arguably something curiously rotten or warped deep down inside most of us; our readiness to lie, to dissimulate, to let our integrity crumble, to avoid speaking the truth.[2]

In the Christian faith, that is called sin and, thankfully, there is a solution for it.

The doctrine of total depravity posits that there is absolutely nothing we can do to save ourselves or to pull ourselves up by our own bootstraps. Any salvation comes from God and God alone, never through our own efforts. God's grace is held out to us in the cross and resurrection of Jesus Christ alone, and not through anything we do ourselves.

That's good news for failures and, when I'm having a bad day, it's a very appealing proposition. I can do nothing to save myself but must rely completely on the saving work of Christ. Is that just a lazy and negative way of seeing human nature, though? Aren't people inherently good, really, deep down inside, not inherently bad? Shouldn't we just work to bring out the good in all of us and stop talking about sin?

This chapter will look at the ultimate human failure, which Christian tradition has termed 'sin'. What is sin? What does it mean to be sinful? And is that the same as committing sins? How sinful are human beings really? It seems to me that unless we understand a bit more about sin, we won't really get to the heart of what it means to fail and to get up again and what it means to be human beings who learn from their mistakes. It's the *perspective* sin gives us that we need most. If all human beings are totally sinful and there is no hope of redemption, then we may as well give up now and let the world go to hell in a handcart. But if God somehow entered our world to deal with our sins, to deal with our sinfulness and our failings and our fallen human nature, and died to make it possible to redeem it, then there is hope. Always hope.

Come back sin, all is forgiven

'Sin' is a word and a concept that has found its way into popular culture. Yet, far from being a depiction of the total and utter depravity of the human condition, it has come to be associated with eating something you probably shouldn't or telling a little fib or indulging in something that is off limits but really rather fun. Google images of 'sin' and you'll see what I mean. (Or maybe don't.)

When we talk about sin these days, therefore, we are no longer likely to be speaking about alienation from Christ and the depravity of our souls. We're more likely to be confessing to eating too much ice-cream. John Portmann writes about this downgrading of sin in modern culture in his *A History of Sin*: 'Now defanged, sin fails to strike fear into the hearts of many religious believers: the West has venialized sin, stripped of its awful glory.'[3]

This leads us to ask, 'Are people really totally good or really totally bad?' The tendency of social media accounts to show only the good parts of our lives means that we're likely to categorize people quickly into one of two camps: People I Agree With and People I Don't. Those we place on pedestals one day can very quickly become the devil incarnate when they say or do something with which popular opinion disagrees or thinks is Very Bad. Cancel culture means that once someone has expressed an opinion that causes offence (to someone, anyone at all), they are instantly cast into outer darkness where there is wailing and gnashing of teeth. Or at least de-platformed from an event.

In relation to children, the pendulum has swung from seeing all little children as inveterate baddies, needing to be trained in godliness, to seeing them as little angels, never being able to do any wrong. 'What? My little Johnny? Let them run around making that godawful noise like a banshee. They're not hurting anyone are they?' I wonder if this has resulted in a 'because you're worth it' generation that is more likely to express its need to be understood than its need to be forgiven.

Maybe it's not that simple. Perhaps we are all a mix of dust and glory. Of course, children are neither 'bad' nor 'good' but a wonderful mix of both. The categories of 'badness' or 'goodness' aren't really appropriate anyway. Our society and culture might have a tendency to see people as either sheep or goats but, in reality, when it comes to sinfulness, we're all some kind of sheepy-goaty hybrid (if such a thing exists). The dividing line between good and evil is not between people but within each person. Aleksandr Solzhenitsyn said:

> The line separating good and evil passes not through states, nor between classes, nor between political parties either – but right through every human heart – and through all human hearts. This line shifts. Inside us, it oscillates with the years. And even within hearts overwhelmed by evil, one small bridgehead of good is retained.[4]

A brief history of sin

So what is sin anyway and who invented it?

The question of when and how sin first entered into the human experience is one that has preoccupied theologians and philosophers since time immemorial. Was the introduction of sin into the pristine perfection of the Garden of Eden the fault of Adam who ate the apple or Eve who gave it to him? Or God, who made them with free will? Or the serpent who persuaded them? Or God, who created the serpent?

To ask where sin originated is to fall into the trap of thinking that all sin is 'someone's fault', which, as we will see, is not really the point. At its heart, sin is about a fractured relationship, and when relationships go wrong there is almost always a panoply of reasons for it. The Rite of Penance in the Catholic Church refers to sin as 'an offence against God which disrupts our friendship with him'.[5] Descriptions of sin in the Bible reflect the multifarious nature of this breakdown of the relationship between God and humanity, between humans and other humans, and between humans and the rest of creation.

Sin in the Old Testament is invariably presented as a rupturing of the 'very good' relationship originally enjoyed between God and humans, and between humans. The destructive effects of that rebellion against God can be seen writ large through the pages of the Hebrew Bible as, again and again, God's people turn from him to worship other gods and to follow their own sinful ways. The effect of this sin is to cause God to grieve, to judge and to seek to call his people back, again and again, back to the holiness that is his and could be theirs: 'If my people who are called by my name humble themselves, pray, seek my face, and turn from their wicked ways, then I will hear from heaven, and will forgive their sin and heal their land' (2 Chronicles 7.14). The means by which God provided for the atonement of the sins of his people in the Old Testament was the system of priestly offerings, which took the form of animal sacrifices. That system was made obsolete by the ultimate sacrifice Jesus made once and for all for everyone's sins when he died on the cross, fulfilling a promise foretold throughout the Old Testament and by the prophets.

Sin doesn't feature quite as much in the Gospels as you might imagine it would. It's well known that Jesus spoke more about money than he did about sin (the two may, of course, be connected). The main framework for under-standing sin in the Gospels, as with Jesus' ministry as a whole, is the kingdom of God – the coming, but not yet complete, rule and reign of God, 'come near' in the life, death and resurrection of Jesus, which will not be fulfilled until the end of time, in the age to come, when God's ways will prevail on earth and there will be no more tears, death, illness, pain, suffering – or sin.

In the very act of announcing the kingdom of God, Jesus put repentance for sin at its core: 'The time is fulfilled, and the kingdom of God has come near; *repent*, and believe in the good news' (Mark 1.15, my italics). Thus, 'God's kingdom, instantiated by Jesus is God's merciful power to rectify a corrupted creation, to put in right relationship with God all that has been fractured and divorced from its Creator.'[6]

Jesus was clear about sin and its effects, and clear about the need for repentance, but he was equally clear about the almost outrageous compassion, love and mercy of God. Like a woman who rejoices over a lost coin or a father who catches a glimpse of his repentant son while he is still a very long way off and runs to fling his arms around him and welcome him home. We will return to look in further detail at the way in which Jesus himself encountered and spent time with sinners in Chapter 5, but for now we note that the way the Gospels present sin is as a fracture, a crookedness in humanity's relationship with God, gently and lovingly restored one sinner at a time through the life, death and resurrection of Jesus.

People often think of sin when they think of St Paul and maybe deservedly so. If you think of the most commonly quoted Bible verses about sin, you'll probably recall excerpts from the writings of Paul: 'all have sinned and fall short of the glory of God' (Romans 3.23); 'The saying is sure and worthy of full acceptance, that Christ Jesus came into the world to save sinners' (1 Timothy 1.15); 'For the wages of sin is death, but the free gift of God is eternal life in Christ Jesus our Lord' (Romans 6.23). The primary word used for sin in the New Testament is *hamartia*, literally 'missing the mark'. The word *hamartia* or derivatives of it occur 37 times in Paul's letter to the Romans alone.[7] Paul envisages sin as a cosmic force for evil, a corruption of the goodness of creation, a disrupter of the relationship between God and humanity, and a destroyer of community. Yet, the presence of sin in the world simply shows the love and power of God to save his people from sin through Christ.

Original sin

One of the questions that has perplexed Christian thinkers throughout the centuries is whether we are born sinful or become so. It is St Augustine who is most associated with the concept of 'original sin'. This is the belief that the sin committed by Adam and Eve when they disobeyed God and ate the forbidden fruit affected not only them, resulting in their ostracization by God and their banishment from the garden, but also travelled down through the generations, affecting every human being born since. That is, all of us. Ian McFarland explains that:

> the doctrine of original sin holds that human moral failing is not something that takes place over time through an individual's committing evil deeds, but is rather a congenital state that renders such deeds inevitable. It teaches that sin is at bottom a matter of being rather than doing, such that we are not sinners because we commit sins; rather, we commit sins because we are already sinners.[8]

Therefore, it is said, all human beings are sinful, even the most innocent-seeming baby. In contrast to the views of Augustine, Pelagius argued that, instead, humans are blank slates responsible for their own nature, so 'all people retained freedom to choose good or evil'[9] and Adam and Eve's sin affected them alone. It's a 'glass wholly full' view of humanity in which human beings are said to have the free will to choose not to sin.

Basil the Great held an even more positive view, that all humans have within them, implanted by God, a 'spark of divine love'. He defined sin as a corruption of our innate power to love and do good. Sin, therefore, is 'the misuse of powers given us by God for doing good', a use contrary to God's commands.[10]

Augustine, however, held that, ultimately, sin is a corruption of the desires, the 'loves' of a person. The love in which God has created human beings for himself turns in on the subject. For Augustine, then, sin is 'love of oneself even to contempt of God'.[11] When Adam and Eve disobeyed God's command, their God-given sensual desire (in this case for satisfaction through food) was corrupted. Sin, says Augustine, is a misdirection of that deep-seated desire given by, and ultimately directed towards, God, and a turning in on itself of the human will. Thus, 'after the fall, every person's loves – good intentions notwithstanding – are misdirected *carnaliter* and people act accordingly. What moves the person is not what she knows, but what she wants'.[12] The word for this is *concupiscence*, which means the corruption and turning inwards of our desires. It is a predicament best expressed by Paul when he wrote to the Romans:

> I do not understand my own actions. For I do not do what I want, but I do the very thing I hate. Now if I do what I do not want, I agree that the law is good. But in fact it is no longer I that do it, but sin that dwells within me. For I know that nothing good dwells within me, that is, in my flesh. I can will what is right, but I cannot do it. For I do not do the good I want, but the evil I do not want is what I do. Now if I do what I do not want, it is no longer I that do it, but the sin that dwells within me.
> (Romans 7.15–20)

Augustine believed that sex was the seat of sinfulness because, in the act of sexual gratification, the will, the desire, overcomes the rational mind. The mechanism by which sin is passed from one generation to each other, therefore, is the very act of sexual intercourse, which, of course, is necessary to create new humans. That means all human beings, from birth, are sinful. It's a view that finds its justification in texts such as Psalm 51:

> For I know my transgressions,
>   and my sin is ever before me.
> Against you, you alone, have I sinned,
>   and done what is evil in your sight,
> so that you are justified in your
>   sentence
>   and blameless when you pass
>   judgement.
> Indeed, I was born guilty,
>   a sinner when my mother
>   conceived me.
> (Psalm 51.3–5)

Because of this, the entire human race is afflicted with corruption and is therefore in need of God's saving grace, wrought wholly and entirely by Jesus Christ's death and resurrection, not by any human effort. As Romans 5.12 puts it, 'Therefore, . . . sin came into the world through one man, and death came through sin, and so death spread to all because all have sinned'. Augustine writes:

> the whole of mankind is a condemned lump (*massa perditionis*), for he who committed the first sin was punished, and along with him all the stock which has its roots in him. The result is that there is no escape for

anyone from this justly deserved punishment, except by merciful and undeserved grace.[13]

That's where the good news comes in. Even though sin has corrupted all people for all time, as the view goes, so also the grace and redemption of Christ is available for all people for all time, 'for as all die in Adam, so all will be made alive in Christ' (1 Corinthians 15.22).

So what does this mean for individuals, the 'one man' (or woman)? I know very well that I am, to use Luther's words, 'quite a sinner', perfectly capable of all sorts of misdemeanours on a daily basis. Yet, if I am predisposed by the sinfulness of my forebears, going right the way back to Eden, does this fact absolve me of individual blame, being, as I am, simply part of a system infected with sin at its very core? If anyone is to blame, surely it's all of us, right?

I sin, you sin, we all sin

In the history of the Christian understanding of sin, a distinction is made between 'sins of commission' and 'sins of 'omission'. 'Sins of commission' are those knowingly committed.

'Sins of omission' are failing to do what you know to be right and is your responsibility or duty to do, because you are afraid or think that it's someone else's problem or, quite frankly, can't be bothered. An example of a sin of omission would be witnessing a crime and failing to do anything about it, such as to report it to the police or step in to help the victim. To get to the heart of sins of omission we need to understand the concept of 'duty'. What duty do we owe God, our fellow human beings and even ourselves?

In the Second World War, Coventry Cathedral was all but destroyed by German bombers. The cathedral has turned its damaged history to good, becoming a centre for reconciliation and the home of the Community of the Cross of Nails, a worldwide network of churches, charities, training organizations, chaplaincies and schools that, 'share a common commitment to work and pray for peace, justice and reconciliation'.[14] The 'Coventry litany of reconciliation', which was written by Canon Joseph Poole in 1958, is prayed every weekday and lays before God a series of sins and failings:

> The hatred which divides nation from nation, race from race, class from class.
> The covetous desires of people and nations to possess what is not their own.
> The greed which exploits the work of human hands and lays waste the earth.
> Our envy of the welfare and happiness of others.
> Our indifference to the plight of the imprisoned, the homeless, the refugee.
> The lust which dishonours the bodies of men, women and children.
> The pride which leads us to trust in ourselves and not in God.[15]

It is significant that the response after each of these penitential sentences is not 'Father, forgive *them*', echoing Jesus' words from the cross (Luke 23.34), but 'Father, forgive'. Full stop. That is because it is not only 'them' God needs to forgive but 'us'. Me too. All of us. We are all sinners. We are all complicit.

So is sin individual or corporate? Is it the case that I, weak and depraved human that I am, choose daily to commit individual acts of wrongdoing because there is a war between my desires going on somewhere inside, and Jesus doesn't always get the final say? Or is sin, rather, something that pervades the whole of the created order, the whole cosmos, with the awful effects of Adam and Eve's first transgression being such that the whole of creation is broken and so we see earthquakes and disease and a seething mass of moral failure? Is it the case that so all-pervasive is sin that to try not to sin in a sinful world is to be doomed to fail? How personally responsible am I for my sins?

One of the things that we've learnt during the pandemic is that we don't exist in isolation from one another (despite the need sometimes to self-isolate). Our individual actions have effects on others. Scientific evidence showed that the wearing of masks during a pandemic, for example, is more likely to protect others from catching COVID from you than it is to stop you catching it from them. The pandemic has taught us that it is not possible to be an island, and all our actions and intentions are interrelated. So how far is sin something we are bound up in simply by being a member of the human race?

I recall one hot summer weekend during the first lock-down, at a time when a two-metre distance between people was being adhered to, and a call went out to discourage people from visiting a local seaside beauty spot because the beaches were becoming crowded and so had become unsafe, in COVID distancing terms. The message on local media was, 'Please refrain from flocking to the beach.' Much as I understood and appreciated the sentiment, this struck me at the time as somewhat odd. It is not possible to 'flock' on your own. If I had wanted to go to the beach, how would I know if others had also decided to that day? Did the beachgoers get up that morning and decide to 'flock'? 'Flocking' is not something that an individual can do alone; it describes a corporate action. What if I had simply decided to go to the beach and others had, too, and we inadvertently found ourselves 'flocking' together by mistake? In pandemics, as in so many other areas of life, we are connected to one another even by seemingly individual actions and their consequences. One person hears a rumour that toilet rolls might be about to run out and so buys an extra packet or two when shopping that day, and so does everyone else and, before you know it, there are no toilet rolls to be found anywhere. One woman decided to stand on her doorstep in London at 8 p.m. every Thursday to clap for key workers, as people were doing in Europe, posted her intention on Twitter and, before long, everyone was out there, banging on saucepans. We are a 'flocking' people, even if we don't set out to be.

It is the same with sin. We take individual responsibility for our own sins, yet we are part of a system, a world in which sinfulness is inherent and we can never escape from it or its effects, no matter how hard we try not to 'flock'.

When people find themselves adrift and end up sleeping on the streets, addicted to crack cocaine and committing crimes to fund their habit, do they do so because they are not taking sufficient responsibility for their own actions and choosing to do bad things or are they the product of sinful systems and cultures – the lack of affordable housing caused by greedy landlords, drug trafficking and the strings of people profiting from it in faraway countries, the lack of investment in our social care system and so on? Are drug dealers evil people or have they been dealt a rough deal in life and are the product of, for example, a chaotic upbringing, inhuman living conditions and an economic system that makes it impossible for people from some sections of society to better themselves and make wise choices? Is it a bit of both?

If we understand all creation as being in a fallen state, then individual human beings are part and parcel of that fallenness. Does that mean we are let off the hook and don't need to take individual responsibility for the things we do wrong? Are people a result simply of the badness that is in the world, in societies and in individual circumstances? How much personal responsibility do we or should we take for our failings?

The Bible would find the question as to whether sin is corporate or individual rather odd, as the two are inextricably linked. Paul writing to the Romans, for example, makes the link between the sin of the one Adam and the sin of the many (the rest of us): 'Therefore, . . . sin came into the world through one man, and death came through sin, and so death spread to all because all have sinned' (Romans 5.12). Likewise, the beneficial effects of the redemption brought about by one man (Jesus) spread to the many (all Christians): 'Therefore just as one man's trespass led to condemnation for all, so one man's act of righteousness leads to justification and life for all. For just as by the one man's disobedience the many were made sinners, so by the one man's obedience the many will be made righteous' (Romans 5.18–19).

Portmann traces the changing patterns of thinking and acting in relation to sin and, through the centuries, it is clear that societies change their perceptions of what is considered sinful and what the consequences of sin ought to be. He says:

> Modern sins seem capable of uniting a variety of people of different religions and ethnic backgrounds. These sins include harming the environment, engaging in racism, denying the Holocaust, being depressed and not seeking pharmacological relief, not reaching your potential and being overweight. Modern sins have increasingly switched the focus from individuals to institutions.[16]

One of the major changes in the way in which sin is viewed, he says, is that we are now far more likely than we were to be aware of the nature of corporate sin and, correspondingly, less bothered about individual moral misdemeanours: 'Because of a deepening sense of justice, Christians are slowly becoming aware that personal sins have social consequences and that the two are reciprocal.'[17]

Sin, therefore, is not only individual and corporate but can also be structural. John Navone defines sinful structures as: 'those elements of established political, social, economic, or cultural systems and institutions that are morally corrupt and corrupting. They directly cause or occasion poverty, injustice, discrimination, and a loss of human dignity and freedom.'[18]

In particular, campaigns against racial injustice have shown us that, although we may not personally enslave fellow humans, the term 'white privilege' applies as there is still an advantage afforded to white people by structures and systems that have traditionally favoured them over their black and brown siblings. In that sense, we are all complicit in the structural sins of our forebears. Jeremy Bergen states, in connection with racism:

> The concept of structural or social sin, employed to describe this reality [racism], refers not primarily to the effect that an individual's sin has on others, but to the fact that there is a dimension of sin which is more than the sum of individual sins. This does not deny personal responsibility, but suggests that the personal is not the only dimension in need of conversion.[19]

Dietrich Bonhoeffer addresses the conundrum of personal versus corporate sin in relation to the Church in his unfinished book *Ethics*. Taking as a starting point the Ten Commandments, he says that sins committed by an individual come to 'infect' the Church and society. Thus, the Church, as 'Christ existing in community must bear the weight of sin in the world, because uniquely in the world only the church knows the depths of all sin as offence against Christ. Through this vicarious action, the church witnesses to Christ, whose forgiveness and call to discipleship is the world's hope.'[20] It is the Church, therefore, that is best placed to acknowledge, account for, repent of and offer reparative action for the sins of the world. In this sense, the Church should be the 'sorriest' institution around.

Given that it involves all of us, here are some thoughts on how to be a truly great sinner.

How to sin really well

Admit, that you are 'quite a sinner'

The New Testament is clear on this, 'If we say that we have no sin, we deceive ourselves, and the truth is not in us' (1 John 1.8). Yet, as we've seen, sin is somewhat out of fashion these days. Jewish scholar Paula Fredriksen, in her work looking at the history of sin, writes:

> Sin and its various historical entailments – guilt, remorse, judgement, punishment, penance, atonement – seem to sit athwart contemporary sensibilities . . . People may not 'believe' in sin, and they may be convinced that while they themselves might 'make mistakes' they do not 'really' sin; but they somehow seem to know sin when they see it in the behaviour of others.[21]

This book is all about failure. If we see sin as the ultimate failure, then admitting we're all sinners is not a bad place to start in coming to terms with how to live with failure well. Indeed, it may be a liberation. To admit that we commit sins, we are part of sinful humanity, we are all sinners, is to join in what Bonhoeffer calls 'the fellowship of the undevout'[22] – those who are so aware of their own failure and need of redemption that pretence is not required and the mercy and grace of God takes centre stage.

Francis Spufford describes 'sin' as the 'human propensity to f**k things up' (HPtFtU) and says:

> You can get quite a long way through an adult life without having to acknowledge your own personal propensity to (etc etc); maybe even all the way through, if you're someone with a very high threshold of obliviousness, or with the kind of disposition that registers sunshine even when a storm is howling all around. But for most of us the point eventually arrives when, at least for an hour or a day or a season, we find we have to take notice of our HPtFtU (as I think I'd better call it).[23]

As I have said, embracing this truth should come as a liberation not a condemnation. Once we acknowledge and accept that we are sinful human beings, we can stop trying to redeem ourselves and working incredibly much harder at being good, to earn our way into heaven by our own goodness. That's just exhausting. Tish Warren writes movingly of when it began to dawn on her that she was not as perfect as the image she tried to present, and how freeing this was for her:

> Far from being a crushing blow of self-hatred, the realization of my actual, non-theoretical sinfulness came with something like a recognition of grace. I saw that I was worse than I'd thought I was, and that truth knocked me off the eternal treadmill of trying to be better and do better and get it all right. It allowed me to slowly (and continually) learn to receive love, atonement, forgiveness and mercy.[24]

Sinfulness – and the fact that you are quite a sinner – is like one of those optical illusions in which a picture can look simultaneously to some people like a duck and to others like a rabbit. You imagine all your life that there is only a duck, but once the rabbit is pointed out to you – 'Yes, look, can't you see? There's its ear . . . ' – or possibly hoves into view all by itself and, either way, your eyes are opened, there is no unseeing it. That is especially true for those of us who call ourselves Christian. Because of the testimony of Christ, none of us can labour under the illusion that we are not sinners. Jesus himself laid this out plainly in his farewell discourse to his disciples: 'If I had not come and spoken to them, they would not have sin; but now they have no excuse for their sin' (John 15.22).

As we saw earlier in this chapter, Jesus spoke surprisingly little of sin, but when he did, his fiercest opprobrium was reserved for those, like the religious leaders, whom he called hypocrites:

Woe to you, scribes and Pharisees, hypocrites! For you are like whitewashed tombs, which on the outside look beautiful, but inside are full of the bones of the dead and of all kinds of filth. So you also on the outside look righteous to others, but inside you are full of hypocrisy and lawlessness.
(Matthew 23.27–28)

The source of their hypocrisy, it seems, was that they failed to recognize their own sinfulness, or at least admit to it, while at the same time decrying everyone else for theirs. Jesus probably spoke in Aramaic, but the Gospels were translated into Greek and the Greek word for 'hypocrite' derives from the word for an 'actor' – literally, the one who was an 'interpreter from underneath [a mask]', the one who pretends to be something he or she is not. So perhaps the first step in being a really successful sinner is to stop acting and admit what you are. Jesus' words are actually very good news for those of us who know and admit that we're failures – we're halfway there already! At least we are aware of our sinfulness.

Acknowledging our sinfulness enables us to do at least three things. First, it unites us with everyone else. Of all the identities we tend to want to give ourselves, 'sinner' is perhaps the most accurate and the most collegial. Owning the title 'sinner' gives us an identity that belongs alongside all the massed ranks of sinners. 'Have mercy on me, a sinner.'

Second, it enables us to see one another as sinners, too, and, therefore, to offer forgiveness and redemption to those who fall short. None of us is perfect and none of us is irredeemable. Bonhoeffer says that the failure to both admit our own sinfulness and to allow others to do the same is the source of hindrance in building the Christian community:

> The final break-through to fellowship does not occur, because, though they have fellowship with one another as believers and as devout people, they do not have fellowship as the undevout, as sinners. The pious fellowship permits no one to be a sinner. So everybody must conceal his sin from himself and from the fellowship. We dare not be sinners. Many Christians are unthinkably horrified when a real sinner is suddenly discovered among the righteous. So we remain alone with our sin, living in lies and hypocrisy. The fact is that we are sinners![25]

Admitting our sin is the key to a breakthrough in fellowship.

Third, it releases us from the obligation to try to be, or look as though we are, perfect. As any addict knows only too well, admitting that you have a problem is the first step towards sorting it out:

> Alas sinfulness is the best we can do. That useful insight can prevent plenty of hand-wringing down the road . . . We do well to turn away from utopian fantasies that don't resemble any possible real world of human behaviour. By predicting regular failures in the game of virtue, we acknowledge our limitations.[26]

To return to the question we asked earlier, if the doctrine of original sin is to be believed, then in what sense am I to be understood as responsible for my own sinfulness or, even more, my own sins? Doesn't original sin fatally undermine the concept of free will and the freedom to choose right from wrong that are so dear to Western civilization?

Ian McFarland offers an alternative view. So greatly has sin corrupted our capacities as a human race, we are not even able to *choose* properly:

> Does this mean that our freedom is an illusion? Yes, if freedom means the capacity to choose our destiny after a manner of the consumer, sovereignly surveying good and evil as we would different brands of mouth-wash . . . Far from causing us to despair this ought instead to cause us to rejoice, for since we are unable not only to save ourselves but even to see our need of salvation clearly, our dependency on God is thrown into even starker relief knowing that though our inca-pacity is deep, the grace of Christ is deeper still, and its power is made perfect in weakness (2 Cor. 12.9).[27]

In the Christian tradition, admitting that you are quite a sinner is called confession – admitting our failures to God and perhaps even to one another. In the psalms, 'Repentance and confession are the means of overcoming sin.'[28] The psalmist also describes the agony of unconfessed sin, followed by the relief that comes when the sinner owns up:

While I kept silence, my body wasted
    away
   through my groaning all day long.
For day and night your hand was
     heavy upon me;
   my strength was dried up as by the
      heat of summer.

Then I acknowledged my sin to you,
   and I did not hide my iniquity;
I said, 'I will confess my
     transgressions to the LORD',
   and you forgave the guilt of my sin.
(Psalm 32.3–5)

Get into training

Since we're on the subject of archaic terms that have gone out of fashion, let's try another one: 'sanctification'. Although I am indeed 'quite a sinner', I am a sinner beloved by God, in whom dwells God's Holy Spirit, whose job it is (among other things) daily to make me more like Jesus – that is, less sinful. That's the process of 'sanctification', which is freeing from sin or becoming holy. Once we have recognized that we are sinners and have begun to repent, sanctification is the ongoing movement of our Christian heart towards a greater love of God and to living more closely in the ways of his kingdom. Bonhoeffer expresses it like this: 'Sanctification means that the Christians have been judged already, and that they are being preserved until the coming of Christ and are ever advancing towards it.'[29] Increasingly, the Christian thinks and speaks and acts and imagines in ways that are morally right. For Bonhoeffer this process became enmeshed with his deliberations about whether or not it was right to oppose the Nazi regime by direct action and to take on himself the possible guilt of such action. Not to do so, for him, would have been a sin of omission.

One of my favourite definitions of Christian maturity is found in Hebrews 5.14: 'those whose faculties have been trained by practice to distinguish good from evil'. That is an accurate summary of sanctification – the constant working of the Holy Spirit of God in the life of believers, such that they become more like Christ and, therefore, better able to distinguish good from evil.

How long does that take? A lifetime. It doesn't mean that you are sin-free, but you come to be trained to recognize your faults and failings. It's what self-help gurus might call self-awareness, but with the added advantage of a trainer from heaven who is able to help you to do something about what you see.

We will never be perfect this side of heaven. The knowledge of that truth used to lead people to be baptized only on their death bed, so afraid were they that they would sin after their baptism and put themselves in a place of eternal damnation. Although we may now think that sounds a bit ridiculous, perhaps they were on to something. Perhaps they realized something quite important, albeit they came up with the wrong remedy. They realized that sinfulness is a part of life that we can never get rid of, so we'd better learn to live with it instead.

What is the 'practice' that Hebrews 5.14 recommends? Sanctification, which is training by the Holy Spirit working in partnership with us to help us to sin less. That training is hard work, happening in the real world with real people. It's not the spiritual equivalent of sitting on a sunbed, waiting for the Holy Spirit to evoke a warm glow from within. It's more like training in a gym, involving puffing, panting and sweating like a horse, and acting, often against our inherent desires, we practise, again and again, including failing and trying again, to be more Christlike.

Dallas Willard defines sanctification as 'a consciously chosen and sustained relationship of interaction between the Lord and his apprentice, in which the apprentice is able to do, and routinely does, what he or she knows to be right before God'.[30] How do we enter into and sustain such training? It's really a matter of taming our desires, disordered, as we have seen, from the very beginning by sin, so that they become reordered to work towards and in alignment with the ways of the kingdom of God.

How do we do that? The answer, I believe, is slightly surprising and maybe not a little unpopular in today's fast-track, shortcut world, where I can have anything I want, whenever I want it, immediately. The answer lies in what we do with our habits. To use the correct terminology, it has to do with spiritual disciplines. Willard puts it like this: 'Our plan for a life of growth in the life of the kingdom of God must be structured around disciplines for the spiritual life.' He defines these disciplines as 'an activity within our power – something we can do – that brings us to the point where we can do what we at present cannot do by direct effort'.[31]

As human beings, we carry a mixed bag of desires with us, some of them godly and some quite the opposite, affected as they are by sin. We *desire* our way around the world and we make choices accordingly. James K. A. Smith, drawing on Augustine, says, 'To be human is to love, and it is what we love that defines who we are.'[32] It's a view that lies behind Augustine's famous prayer: 'O God you have made us for ourselves and our hearts are restless until they find their rest in you.'[33] What we need to do, therefore, is train our desires to be more in tune with the heart of God and his kingdom. Disciplines and spiritual habits help to sharpen the focus of where we set our affections.

Lent is the time when Christians are encouraged to 'turn away from sin and be faithful to Christ'. A mark of this intention is smeared on our foreheads on Ash Wednesday, when a sign of the cross is made using the burnt remains of Palm Sunday crosses from the year before. To signify this change of heart, many people give things up – alcohol, chocolate, certain meals, social media. Some take things up instead – times of silence, charitable giving and so on. These spiritual disciplines train our desires to be more in line with a faithfulness to Christ and less in line with our own sinful cravings. But, being human, we keep defaulting to the false norths of all our failings. Every time we resist something we could have – a meal, a glass of wine, a bar of chocolate, busyness, TV, the Internet, social media – we live into that yearning reality. Willard summarizes the difficulty of this training for godliness:

Often when we come to do the right thing we have already done the wrong thing, because that is what was sitting in our body 'at the ready.' Intention alone cannot suffice in most situations where we find ourselves. We must be 'in shape.' If not, trying will normally be too late, or totally absent. Instead, our intention and effort must be carried into effect by training which leaves our body poised to do what Christ would do, well before the occasion arises. Such training is supplied by the disciplines for life in the Spirit.[34]

So, when we fast from something or deny ourselves something, we are saying that things are not as they should be; we are mourning the not yet, the presence of evil in the world – and in ourselves – and we are asking God to use us to do something about it. Spiritual disciplines such as fasting are practices and habits that orientate our hearts and minds to see past the distractions of our cultures and uncover the heart of God.

Sin big

One of the greatest deficiencies of the human condition is that we imagine our sins are small. The cognitive dissonance we experience daily – 'I am a good person, I deserve more, I am worth it, so why do I keep doing and saying and thinking bad things and why do bad things keep happening to me?' – comes about because we tend to say that we have no sin and so the truth is not in us. 'Sin? Me? No, surely not!'

Coupled with that, when we do admit we are sinners (because we know it to be true deep down), we think we can't be *that* bad. But to minimize our sins (or, perhaps more accurately, our sinfulness) has several effects. One is that when we do sin big, we're shocked and feel even more like failures. Another is that it leads us to be more judgemental of others. As we saw in Edmondson's research, we tend to self-justify, giving reasons for why we got things wrong – 'It was because of circumstances', 'I couldn't help it', 'Everything was stacked against me', 'It was someone else's fault' – yet tend to do the opposite with the sins of others, assigning fault to them much more readily – 'I can't believe they did that!' A third effect is that we tend to excuse ourselves from the part we play in the sinfulness of humanity as a whole.

To counter these effects, we need to own our part in the big sins of the world. Sin is both a power and a behaviour. We neither need, nor are able to, choose between the two or prioritize one over the other. Stephen Ray defines structural or systemic sin as a 'dimension of sin – while emanating as all sin does from the doings of human beings – [that] specifically refers to workings of sin in the world in magnitudes beyond the scope of individual actions'.[35] He says that this kind of sin is when it becomes 'mundane', but we need to recognize that it:

> can so inundate the fabric of things that every thought, every action, and the material conditions under which those thoughts provoke actions *all* proceed along lines that are in place because of the workings of sin.[36]

The most obvious example of this is the way in which the sin of racism has shaped and continues to shape the ordering of our world, particularly in the West. One of the revelations of thinking on racism in more recent years has been that it is insufficient simply to be 'not racist' myself. I must also acknowledge the fact that I live in a society, many of the benefits of which have come about because of a dark history of colonialism, racism and oppression. I am shaped by that history in my thinking and my acting, and I sin accordingly. Hence, theologian Willie James Jennings paints a picture of the impacts of colonialism and racial oppression on the world that he calls Christianity's 'diseased social imagination'. It prevents our faith from being one that:

> understands its own deep wisdom and power in joining, mixing, merging and being changed by multiple ways of life to witness to a God who surprises us by love of differences and draws us to new capacities to imagine their reconciliation.[37]

James Cone, a founder of black liberation theology, encourages his readers to see sin not as individual acts of wrongdoing but as a community concept: 'There can be no knowledge of the sinful condition except in the movement of an oppressed community claiming its freedom.'[38]

What is my responsibility in relation to such structural or systemic sin? Is it possible to be complicit in a sin that you did not yourself commit? Is it possible to repent regarding not only your own sins but also those of the whole world, the sins of all humanity? In admitting that we are quite big sinners in this respect, it would be easy to become overwhelmed and feel inadequate for the task of being able to do anything to address the sinfulness we feel and experience in relation to systemic sin. So what to do? How do we play our part in repenting the big sins of the world?

As with sin generally, the first step is awareness. There are moments in history when we need the kind of awakening about the state of the world in which we live that often accompanies tragic events. Cone puts it thus: 'Our survival and liberation depend upon our recognition of the truth when it is spoken and lived by the people. If we cannot recognize the truth, then it cannot liberate us from untruth.'[39]

I grew up in a fairly conservative church where women were not allowed to exercise leadership. I thought that was just the way the world was. I recall vividly my awakening to an alternative possibility that came from reading feminist writings on the power of language to shape reality as part of my linguistics course at university. Deborah Cameron's *The Myth of Mars and Venus* opened my eyes to a new way of seeing the world and the structural sin of misogyny in a way that has shaped my life and ministry ever since. The murder of George Floyd and the subsequent Black Lives Matter movement was another such opportunity to wake up and see things the way they really are. There have been and will be other such moments.

The second step is to acknowledge the need to listen and understand. Cone writes powerfully about how white people are not able to comment on the sins and experiences of black people: 'Only blacks can speak about God in relationship to their liberation.'[40] We must listen carefully first, if we are to understand.

The third, possibly somewhat paradoxical step is that there is a need to speak out about what we now know to be wrong and sinful. We should acknowledge that this is difficult, particularly regarding the intersection between the second step – listening and understanding – and this third one – speaking out.

Some would have you speak before you are ready. 'Silence is complicity,' they say. Church leaders especially are accused of this if they do not immediately, decisively and vehemently comment on any injustice/happening/event/form of theology/opinion, preferably on social media in a way deemed acceptable to the angry crowd. 'Your silence is deafening!' comes the cry.

This is a problem. How do we make the public debate a place where people are able to stay silent for as long as it takes to gather all the facts, to do the listening mentioned above and to work things out, but no longer? How do we acknowledge and recognize the time that may need to be taken to wake up, change views, see sin? How do we hold that tension between humility about our changing views, not being pressured into shrill proclamations and yet also having the courage to speak in a timely and courageous manner when we see something that is wrong, lest we fall into sins of omission?

The fourth and final step is acting in small ways. We may not be able to change the world or take on our own shoulders all that is wrong around us, but we can buy eco toilet paper, give to charities that support refugees, write to our MP. I once attended an interview for a job and said to the appointing panel that if I and a person of colour were equally qualified for the job, I hoped they might consider appointing that person over me. They did. It felt like a small victory. In each small act is a confession: 'I am part of this.' There is also repentance: 'And I want to do something about it.'

Develop the forgetfulness of God

Memory plays an important role in repentance, reconciliation and making right past sins: 'Truthful memories are a condition for the redemption of memory and reconciliation . . . Truthful memories must name the wrong done, and name the wrongdoers.'[41] Hence, truth-telling is an important first step in reconciliation after failure, which must involve accurate remembering.

When it comes to how God sees our sins, however, there is an important point to be made about remembering and forgetting. There is a need to remember, but there is also a need to forget – or to not call to mind – 'for if everything were remembered, the entire past would be fully present every moment and as such completely unusable and paralysing'. The important thing with remembering, says Bergen, 'is that memory is like a ladder which can be kicked away once the summit is reached, but it is crucial that the ladder not be kicked away too soon, or by the wrong person.'[42]

Recognizing that we are all sinners brings great freedom, as we have seen, and so also does the knowledge that God does not leave us to wallow in our sins but comes to us in the person of Christ, with grace, mercy and forgiveness. Owning up to our sins is the first step towards forgiveness: 'If we confess our sins, he who is faithful and just will forgive us our sins and cleanse us from all unrighteousness' (1 John 1.9). Once that confession has taken place, however, God does something remarkable with our sins and the memory of them. The psalmist promises that God will take our sins far away from us, 'as far as the east is from the west' (Psalm 103.12). But God goes even further than that. In fact, the Bible shows us a God who is so ready and willing to forgive sins that he can't even remember them half the time: 'I, I am He who blots out your transgressions for my own sake, and I will not remember your sins,' says the prophet Isaiah (43.25). So also does Jeremiah: 'No longer shall they teach one another, or say to each other, "Know the LORD," for they shall all know me, from the least of them to the greatest, says the LORD, for I will forgive their iniquity, and remember their sin no more' (31.34). 'For I will be merciful towards their iniquities, and I will remember their sins no more,' promises the writer of the letter to the Hebrews (8.12). Paul writing to the Romans takes it a step further and says that God will not even consider our sin as sin: 'Blessed are those whose iniquities are forgiven, and whose sins are covered; blessed is the one against whom the Lord will not reckon sin' (4.7–8).

God, then, may be perfect, but he's very forgetful when it comes to our sins, negligent even, in the matter of counting our sins against us. That is a great encouragement to all of us who consider ourselves failures. With the awakening to the knowledge of sin comes inevitable guilt, but even as that happens, God has already provided the solution, and has blotted out our sin. As the great Baptist preacher Charles Spurgeon writes, 'So a man may blot his sins from his memory, and quiet his mind with false hopes, but the peace which this will bring him is widely different from that which arises from God's forgiveness of sin through the satisfaction which Jesus made in his atonement. Our blotting is one thing, God's blotting out is something far higher.'[43] So go, experience the 'blotting out' of God.

A clergy friend of mine went into a local primary school to take an assembly and subjected herself to a grilling by the children. She said that they could ask her any question they wanted to. 'What's the worst sin you've ever committed?' piped up one child. Without missing a beat my friend responded, 'I can't remember – and neither can God.'

For discussion

1 What does 'sin' mean to you? How is the distinction between 'sins of commission' and 'sins of omission' helpful?

2 In what ways do you find it useful to distinguish between individual, corporate and structural sin?

3 What role does confession play in your life?

4

The failing Church

Even in its human weakness, the Church is still the bride of Christ.
Justin Welby, Archbishop of Canterbury, final keynote address to the Lambeth Conference (2022)

What is the Church?

A few years ago, when I was a bishop in Cumbria, I read the book *English Pastoral* by Cumbrian shepherd James Rebanks. It struck me then how much of what Rebanks writes about the state of farming in the twenty-first century strikes a chord with how I feel about the state of the Church, and of ministry within it. He writes:

> I'd always wanted to be the farmer ... but the moment it happened it felt empty. The world seemed a dull shade of grey. Beyond our little valley, people seemed to have gone insane. England was divided and broken. Suddenly in those months I felt lost . . . Being a farmer felt for the first time like something you were supposed to say sorry for.[1]

For 'farmer', read 'vicar' or 'lay leader' or 'bishop'. For 'valley', read 'church'. For 'England', read the 'Church of England'. The Church, like farming, faces a crisis of resources, a crisis of identity and a crisis of confidence. In many ways, the Church is failing, so what to do?

Let me first ask you, how do you feel about the Church right now? No, honestly? Sometimes, on a good day, I am so proud of the Church, even the part of it with which I have most to do – the Church of England. On other days, I could cheerfully dump the whole lot into the pits of hell to be tormented by the devil and all his little minions with their pitchforks for ever and ever, amen.

There are many good things that come to mind for me when I think about the Church – love, friendship, fellowship, worship, compassion, community. Jesus. But there are also some things that get my goat. Now, I could name all sorts of things, like division in the Anglican Communion over the issue of human sexuality, denominational differences that lead us to be out of fellowship with one another, the failures and frustrations and foibles of the institution, the way the Church has colluded with all sorts of heinous practices through the ages. There is one thing, however, that winds me up about the Church above all else. It's that little saucer. It's usually pale green and is put out at coffee time after the service, for people to put money on for their coffee. Except it's quite passive aggressive. There's never a sign that says, 'Coffee costs about 10p per cup for us to make. Please give generously.' The saucer is just left there on the surface, lurking, accusing anyone who dares to take coffee without donating. I call it the Saucer of Doom.

Now, don't get me wrong, I love all those who serve on the coffee rotas in our churches. Thank you. You're amazing. But, why? Why do we do that thing? We invite people to church. They come! It's an actual miracle!! They showed up! 'You're so welcome! It's so good to see you here! Welcome to our church!' *Now give us 10p for your coffee!!!* I know it's well-intentioned. I know coffee is expensive, and electricity, but whenever I see that saucer, I am so tempted to slap down a £20 note and say, 'Thank you. I'll cover everyone this morning. *Now take the saucer away!'*

Anyway, that's just me. You?

The Church is both a human institution, with all the faults and failings human beings can muster together, and an eternal cosmic reality against which our Lord assured us that the very gates of hell will not prevail. When it comes to thinking about failure in the Church, that is a challenging conundrum to navigate.

The sorry litany of individual and corporate failures in the Church is writ large on the pages of history. I hardly need to name them, do I? The way the Church has allowed abuse of all kinds to happen within its walls and spheres of influence, covered it up, then failed to deal well with it when it came to light. The exporting, along with the gospel, on the coat-tails of empire, the worst of Western Christianity's values and norms and the inflicting of awful harm and oppression of many kinds on Indigenous peoples the world over. The perpetuation of patriarchy that kept women out of the pulpit and in the kitchen for generations. The individual foibles, falls and failures of 'celebrity' ministers with all the ensuing pain, hurt and confusion for their families and congregations. And that's just going back a few hundred years. There are others, of course.

Yet, at the heart of the Christian gospel is a powerful message of reconciliation, with God and with one another. That is a statement it is easy to gloss over, but it is profoundly significant. It's tempting to hear talk of reconciliation and imagine that what is being talked about is simply being nice to one another or, possibly, sorting conflicts or intervening when people don't get on. Reconciliation is that but it is also so much more than that. Let's look at why.

One of the most important passages in the Bible when it comes to thinking about the nature of the Church is Ephesians chapter 3, in which Paul explains his 'understanding of the mystery of Christ' (v. 4). What is this 'mystery' that Paul is so keen to reveal to his readers? Simply that Gentile believers have, along with their Jewish siblings, been reconciled to God through the cross of Christ, 'the Gentiles have become fellow-heirs, members of the same body, and sharers in the promise in Christ Jesus through the gospel' (v. 6).

It's quite difficult for us to appreciate fully what a radical new way of thinking that would have represented for Paul's original Jewish readers. It was a major shift in the way that they had thought about life, the universe and everything. It was deeply engrained in their world view that their religion, culture and practices all pointed to them being the only chosen ones, the only heirs of Abraham, God's people. Yet, through the cross of Christ, Paul says, *all* – each and every person and language and people and nation – are now able to be fellow heirs, adopted into God's family, sharing the promises God made to Israel with all his children, reconciled to God and to one another.

So next time I stand in the coffee queue and I spy the Saucer of Doom, I am going to remember Ephesians 3 and thank God that I get to be part of this wonderful thing we call the Church – all God's people reconciled with God and with one another through the death and resurrection of Jesus Christ. Paul's vision is that the Church isn't an optional extra we can add on to a personal faith in Jesus 'if we feel like it'. Membership of the body of Christ, with our siblings, this radical new inclusive community of belonging and reconciliation, is absolutely central to the gospel.

In fact, I would go so far as to say it *is* the gospel. Salvation is not merely personal. Through Jesus' life, death and resurrection, we now have this deep spiritual unity between people of diverse racial, cultural and political backgrounds – what theologian Willie James Jennings calls 'boundary-defying relationships'.[2] It is a completely different way of seeing the entire history of humanity. We tend to think of history as tracing the development of rulers and nations, empires, armies, wars and borders. At least that's what I mostly learnt in my history classes at school. The 'boundary-defying' vision of the Church and history itself that we have been talking about, however, is not about the forming of barriers between people but about removing barriers and breaking down walls between people. It is not about the rise and fall of nations and the mongering of wars, but about the spiritual battles in the heavenly places. It's not about the kings and the queens, emperors and rulers, but about the little people, the 'very least' among the saints. The 'faithful ones' are the real heroes of this story.

So whenever you hear that the Church is irrelevant or has lost its place in society or that no one cares about the Church any more, think of Paul's cosmic vision of the great mystery of God revealed – which brought about the Church. 'Ah, yes,' I hear you cry, 'but have you seen my church? How does this grand vision of the breaking down of the dividing wall of hostility for all time apply to the good people of St Botolph's of Little Puddle? It's all very well to say that we are "sharers in the promise in Christ Jesus through the gospel", but have you met my PCC? Or my vestry meeting or church council or elders? What has this cosmic vision of the Church got to do with my local church?'

I want to answer that by looking at verse 10. In my view, Ephesians 3.10 is a verse that should be emblazoned on the door of every church building, be written into every leadership role description, be the header for every committee discussion document. Paul writes:

Although I am the very least of all the saints, this grace was given to me to bring to the Gentiles the news of the boundless riches of Christ, and to make everyone see what is the plan of the mystery hidden for ages in God, who created all things; *so that through the church the wisdom of God in its rich variety might*

*now be made known to the rulers and authorities in
the heavenly places.*
(Ephesians 3.8–10, italics mine)

Paul was given his ministry to tell the Gentiles that,
through the death and resurrection of Jesus Christ, they
were now included in the Church, 'so that *through the
church* the wisdom of God . . . might now be made known
to the rulers and authorities in the heavenly places'. The
word translated as 'church' in the English Bible – *ekklesia*
– literally means 'the called-out ones' (from the Greek
ek-kaleo). It has its roots in the Hebrew word for the
congregation of Israel – *quahal* – which simply means 'an
assembly', the gathering of those 'called out'. Not called out
to be separate from the world and its problems, but called
out from their homes to gather in a public place. Not called
out *from* the world and all its problems and difficulties but
called out *into* the world.

When we're talking about the Church in relation to
Ephesians, therefore, we are talking about the gathering
of all God's people, called out and saved throughout all
time and history to gather around the throne of Jesus. The
heavenly assembly, the universal, cosmic, multinational,
multiracial, boundaryless community of saved and reconciled people. Through this assembly of called-out ones, the
manifold wisdom of God is made known.

The wisdom of God's wonderful redemption plan is to
unite heaven and earth, and all peoples, through the death
of his son Jesus on the cross. That wisdom is described
as 'manifold' (which is better translated as 'vibrant and

multicoloured') and is elsewhere described as a 'stumbling-block to Jews and foolishness to Gentiles' (1 Corinthians 1.23). This is a topsy-turvy wisdom, where laying down your life is the way to gain it, the ignominious death of the Messiah on a cross is somehow glory and your little, local, weak and broken church, living in the reconciliation wrought by the cross of Christ, is God's best idea to show the world what God is like. In fact, not just show the world but also show the 'rulers and authorities in the heavenly places'. Some translations say the 'powers and principalities'.

What or who the dickens are they?

Powers and principalities

The 'powers' are a spiritual reality beyond what we can see. They are beings who exist in the heavenly realms. In Ephesians 6.12, they are called the 'spiritual forces of evil in the heavenly places'. They are malevolent supernatural forces who have a very visible influence on the course of human history – its people, systems and political structures, and its institutions, including the Church:

> there are individual sins, then there is an individual's struggle against sin, and then there are corporate manifestations of sin, larger than the sum of their parts. Here we have what might be considered an additional layer, or else an explanation behind those other manifestations of sin's power: spiritual forces beyond humanity are at work to pull people away from life and salvation.[3]

Stephen Ray defines such powers and principalities as 'those systems of thought interpretation and material relations that work to impose the dominion of a power upon human reality'.[4] Walter Wink says that they are 'the great socio-spiritual forces that preside over much of reality. I mean the massive institutions, social structures, and systems that dominate our world today, and the spirituality at their center.'[5]

Before we might be tempted to think that all this 'rulers and authorities, powers and principalities' stuff is just hocus-pocus and we know so much more in our modern scientific age, just think about how many of the good and God-inspired inventions of our time can be taken over and used to oppress and terrorize people and communities. Nuclear power, potentially a clean and renewable source of energy, is used by world leaders to threaten one another's very existence. Scientific ingenuity can be used to make vaccines that save millions of lives, but it can also be used to make chemicals which kill innocent people in Syria and Salisbury. Poverty, injustice, greed, lack of opportunity, racial hatred, violence, human trafficking are evidence of spiritual foes at work, often through human agency. We are held hostage by subsystems that we don't even know exist and lead us to see ourselves and other people in ways that diminish God's image in them.

What those powers and principalities seek to do most especially is to undermine the 'mystery hidden for ages in God' (Ephesians 3.9) – that is, the reality of reconciliation between God and humanity and between people, as exemplified by the inclusion of Gentiles in the people of God:

Any earthly division is a demonstration that the principalities and powers are at work, maintaining on earth
the hostility that Jesus' own body destroyed . . . The
work of the principalities and powers, against which
Paul summons people to fight, is first of all the work
of division.[6]

The Church stands to prove that division is not the way of
God. The incredible implication of Ephesians 3.10 is that
God's multicoloured wisdom is shown to these dark forces
through the Church. Yes, that's you and me, folks! *The
Church* is how God chooses to make known the wisdom
of his brilliant plan to redeem the world. It's as though the
Church becomes a lecture theatre in which the rulers and
authorities of this world are made to sit for a lesson on God's
wisdom. It's as though the Church is the picture on the
advertisement billboard past which the powers and principalities drive every day on their way to work. It's as though
the Church is standing atop the victory bus as it is paraded
through the streets with the powers and principalities
looking on. The Church is the means by which God shows
to the hidden forces of this world the wisdom of God's
plan to reconcile all people to himself through the cross of
Christ. The mere existence of the Church demonstrates that
Christ has been victorious.

Note also that what is being 'made known' is not simply
the *fact* of God's plan for redemption but also its *wisdom*.
The way you prove that something was a wise plan is
to show it working. When the Church demonstrates
its unity, therefore, when it rises up to be all it can be,

bringing reconciliation, challenging injustice, heralding freedom, proclaiming good news, when we refuse hostility and division, when we treat one another – everyone – as Christian brothers and sisters, then we show the wisdom of God to the rulers and authorities, *by being the Church Christ died to create.*

Now, if that doesn't transform the way you see the potential of the Church, I don't know what will.

But how does all that tally with the Church we so often see failing? What if you are reading this and thinking, 'That's all very well, but God must have had in mind some other reality called "the Church" that lurks behind the scenes and is a million miles away from ordinary mortals like me or my church, especially St Botolph's in Little Puddle!'

So, here's the news: he doesn't.

There is no ideal church.

Not in reality, nor even in God's mind or God's plan or up God's sleeve. There is no abstract and ideal church that is any different from the church gathering you are part of. All churches are glorious and, at the same time, failing. Most of Paul's letters were written to address failures of different kinds. In fact, it's quite fun to play 'guess the failure' from Paul's responses.

John's letters to the seven churches in Revelation, likewise, identify some kind of failure or problem of their own or another's making (with the possible exception of Smyrna and Philadelphia): 'you have abandoned the love you had at first' (Ephesus, Revelation 2.4); 'you have some there who hold to the teaching of

Balaam' (Pergamum, 2.14); 'you tolerate that woman Jezebel, who calls herself a prophet' (Thyatira, 2.20); 'I have not found your works perfect in the sight of my God' (Sardis, 3.2); 'you are wretched, pitiable, poor, blind, and naked' (Laodicea, 3.17). John wrote all these wonderful words in Revelation to the congregations of real churches in and around Ephesus that were very far from perfect.

Acts 19 shows that the Ephesus church was badly discipled and small. Paul's letters to Timothy, one of the leaders of the Ephesus church, also show that it had its fair share of issues, yet it is precisely to this weak, troubled and failing church that Paul writes his glorious, inspiring words.

From this we can see that it's not like there is a perfect church 'out there' that we just need to find. This is it. *This* is all there is. As Robert Jenson puts it, 'God the Father intends that there be a church and that this church be exactly the one that exists . . . There is no ideal church, only the one that exists.'[7]

So how do we reconcile the amazing, cosmic vision of who and what the Church is with the weak, failing and fallible organization we see in our pews and parsonages, and in the news day after day? Sometimes the powers and principalities have seemed to be more inside the Church, undermining its unity in a self-destructive way, than outside it. How do we continue to live out that beautiful vision of unity and reconciliation held out to us in Ephesians, and how on earth do we decide what we should all do next?

On divisions in the Church

Through the Church, the manifold wisdom of God is made known to the powers and principalities. That's all well and good, but what happens if all we see in the Church is less the 'manifold wisdom of God' and more the 'maniacal willfulness of sinful people intent on division'?

John Navone states that the divided Church is the worst kind of advert for the gospel of Christ:

> Hatred among Christians is the supreme symbol of evil because it deprives others of the authentic revelation of God's love in Christ, because it is the culpable failure to communicate the divine mercy for the fulfilment of others, and because it tends to render the meaning of God in Christ contemptible for others.[8]

Similarly, when Paul wrote to the Galatian Christians about how members of Christ's body, the Church, should act and behave, not only in relation to the rest of the world but with one another, he speaks of the freedom won by the cross of Christ and goes on to say:

> For you were called to freedom, brothers and sisters; only do not use your freedom as an opportunity for self-indulgence, but through love become slaves to one another. For the whole law is summed up in a single commandment, 'You shall love your neighbour as yourself.'
> (Galatians 5.13–14)

He then explains how 'life in the Spirit' enables this loving:

> Live by the Spirit, I say, and do not gratify the desires of the flesh. For what the flesh desires is opposed to the Spirit, and what the Spirit desires is opposed to the flesh; for these are opposed to each other, to prevent you from doing what you want. But if you are led by the Spirit, you are not subject to the law. Now the works of the flesh are obvious: fornication, impurity, licentiousness, idolatry, sorcery, enmities, strife, jealousy, anger, quarrels, dissensions, factions, envy, drunkenness, carousing, and things like these. I am warning you, as I warned you before: those who do such things will not inherit the kingdom of God. (Galatians 5.16–21)

It's the bit just before Paul writes about the fruits of the Spirit that, I have to confess, I have heard many more sermons on than this passage, which precedes it. When we do, rarely, focus on this text, we tend most often to highlight the 'juicy' sins of 'fornication, impurity, licentiousness, idolatry, sorcery . . . drunkenness, carousing' and overlook the more boring-sounding 'relational' sins of 'enmities, strife, jealousy, anger, quarrels, dissensions, factions, envy'. Yet, how often do we see those more mundane sins consuming churches, as people fall out with one another, fail to love others and descend into factions and parties (not the fun kind)?

Paul's words to the Christian community are strong – 'become slaves to one another' – and yet, as a bishop, I reckon that a lot of my time is spent dealing with situations in parishes, churches and communities that show this most certainly has not been the case. The sins of 'communal discord'[9] that Paul lists in Galatians 5 are very much evident in churches of every denomination and flavour. So, let's take a look at each of them and see what they say to us about the failure that is division in the Church.[10]

The first relational sin that Paul names is 'enmities' (in Greek, *echthrai*). The word suggests hostile sentiments that, in turn, lead to hostile acts.[11] Christians will always have those with whom they disagree, or even call enemies, but the call here is to treat one's enemies well, or even to love them, in line with the command of Jesus: 'You have heard that it was said, "You shall love your neighbour and hate your enemy." But I say to you, Love your enemies and pray for those who persecute you' (Matthew 5.43–44).

It's a call to break the pattern of ongoing enmity and to *choose* to relate in a respectful way with those who are our enemies, despite our differences. Walter Wink writes movingly about the 'enemy as a gift', who can teach us something about ourselves, if we allow God to reveal the reason within us, as well as within them, that leads us to see them as enemies in the first place. When we have learnt this, says Wink:

we are able to develop an objective rage at the injustices they have perpetrated while still seeing them as children of God. The energy squandered nursing hatred becomes available to God for confronting the wrong or transforming the relationship.[12]

Seeing our enemies as deluded by the powers and principalities, 'victims of the delusional system', enables us to understand that 'our struggle is not against enemies of blood and flesh, but against the rulers, against the authorities, against the cosmic powers of this present darkness, against the spiritual forces of evil in the heavenly places' (Ephesians 6.12).

'Strife' or 'quarrelsomeness' (*ereis*) is the opposite of peace, personified in Greek mythology as Eris, the goddess of war and discord. In the Church, this kind of strife comes about when the gospel itself, or the way in which we interpret it, becomes the cause of disunity.

Paul would have a lot to say to our churches today when debates about the way in which we interpret the Bible are carried out in a manner antithetical to the key gospel message of love.

'Jealousy' (*zeloi*), again, is not necessarily negative. In other places (such as 2 Corinthians 11.2), Paul speaks of his own zeal for the Church. In this instance, however, he is referring to those times when zeal or passion for a cause, which can be God-given and channelled for great good – most especially the cause of the gospel of Christ – leads us, instead, to become carried away with selfish resentment. When that happens, we are inclined to allow the 'how' of the way we express our zeal to undermine the message of the 'what' we wish to say.

The word for 'anger' (*thumoi*) denotes a sudden outburst of rage – that overly hasty action we take when something gets our goat and we just blow up before knowing all the facts. It's the reason it's always best to wait before writing or sending that angry email or tweet (even though it's annoying to wait because the feeling of indignation leads, I find, to a great eloquence about what I want to say). In my best moments, I try to stop and think about whether the way in which I react to something in the heat of the moment will actually, in the end, take a lot longer to deal with because I will also have to put right its ill effects as well as the thing that originally caused my outburst. As Paul puts it in Ephesians 4.26, using the same word, 'Be angry but do not sin; do not let the sun go down on your anger.'

'Quarrels' (*eritheiai*) is also used elsewhere (Philippians 2.3; James 3.14), in relation to 'selfish ambition'. It has its roots in the actions of those seeking election to political office for their own gain. It represents a kind of passion that focuses on the self rather than on others, which is the thrust of Paul's argument throughout this section.

'Dissensions' (*dichostasiai*) – the Greek word literally means 'two stands' or 'standing apart' – also refers to those times when different parties form on two 'sides' of an argument or disagreement. It relates to disunity in the body of Christ, which, if this list is ever taken at face value, is just as bad as any kind of sexual misdemeanour. The very word 'division' when used in the Church context suggests those occasions when we allow our disagreements to render us asunder from one another – if not formally and structurally, at least in tone or attitude.

One of the most helpful things we can do in debates is to watch our language about disagreement. Even calling different viewpoints 'sides' allows 'dissension' to develop in our minds, which then becomes lived out in our actions and responses.

'Factions' (*haireseis*) occur when people put up barriers around themselves and their views over and against other views. It is determining whom I allow into my grouping and whom I will exclude as heretics ('heretic' coming from the Greek word *haireseis*). It is the 'formation of cliques, with the resultant exhibitions of party spirit'.[13]

One of the key things about the Church is that we don't get to choose our sisters and brothers in Christ. A document on the nature of the Church produced to accompany the Living in Love and Faith process puts it like this: 'to be a friend of Jesus also means to welcome those whom Jesus gives to us to be our friends; those, that is, whom we might not have chosen ourselves otherwise – or even have welcomed as our allies.'[14] Therefore, in relation to our disagreements within the Church:

> it might be conceivable to feel, on the one hand, that our friendship as members of Christ's church has run aground on our disagreement, and yet to believe that we are nonetheless held – and held together – by Jesus' gifts of friendship.[15]

Right from when the Church first formed, it was set apart from the rest of society by this fact that people who didn't normally associate with one another began to see themselves as part of the same body. Hence, we read in Acts 11.26 that 'it was in Antioch that the disciples were first called "Christians"'. What else could this diverse and mixed group of people have been called that would adequately sum up who they were – these people who crossed every social and ethnic boundary, having little in common except their faith in Jesus Christ? Formerly, they would have been known in all sorts of ways. The differences in their identities would have been important, and usually highlighted in their names – Saul of Tarsus, Onesimus the slave – but in Antioch, the Holy Spirit was doing a new thing and bringing people together, for one reason, under one title and with one name: *Christianos*. It was probably a nickname given by others rather than chosen by the Christians themselves, maybe even slightly mocking them, like friends of the Wesleys being called 'Methodists' as an insult.

This new event, this coming together, this overturning of historic and deep-seated divisions by the work of the Holy Spirit was noticed by everyone around and earned itself a name. I wonder if, despite our differences in today's Church, we will earn ourselves the right to be called that name by others? The Church, including the Church of England, is a place wrought with turbulence, challenges and divisions, where people claim for themselves all sorts of different names and titles and identities, saying, 'I am in that group, but not that group.'

God's clearest call to us, too, is to dare to be those brought together by very little other than God's reconciling work on the cross of Christ – to live like this with one another and in the world at large and, in so doing, earn ourselves the name 'Christians'.

'Envy' (*phthonoi*) is jealousy mixed with spite: 'the grudging spirit that cannot bear to contemplate someone else's prosperity'.[16] It's not only wanting what someone else has but also being resentful of someone else's good fortune. It's knowing you're a failure and wanting everyone else to be one too.

Having considered this sobering list of sins in Galatians 5, we find it is mainly about the 'how' rather than the 'what' of relating in the Christian community. Lists of vices and virtues, like this one and those found elsewhere in Paul's letters, were fairly common in writings of the period. They usually included censure of things such as sexual immorality, drunkenness, sorcery, idolatry. But Paul's list stands out for his inclusion of 'enmities, strife, jealousy, anger, quarrels, dissensions, factions, envy' alongside the other more usual 'works of the flesh'. They are there because 'flesh' in Paul does not refer to physicality or 'bodiliness' but is used for all things that are in opposition to the life in the Spirit, to denote rebellion against God.

It seems that the failure the Galatian church was struggling with was the kind of self-righteousness that damages the life of the body of Christ, the Church, every bit as much as carnal sins. Paul's message would seem to be this: how we behave towards one another in the Church (and, yes, even on social media) is as significant as what we say we believe. The way we disagree is as important as what we disagree about. The fact that Paul had occasion to write his list at all shows that the Galatian church in the first century was no different from the ones we belong to today. Paul's words are harsh – those who continually practise such things won't be seen as children of a heavenly Father, who could not be further away from such behaviours, so they won't be seen as inheritors of his kingdom. The antidote – life in the Spirit – is exemplified by the list that follows:

> By contrast, the fruit of the Spirit is love, joy, peace, patience, kindness, generosity, faithfulness, gentleness, and self-control. There is no law against such things. And those who belong to Christ Jesus have crucified the flesh with its passions and desires. If we live by the Spirit, let us also be guided by the Spirit. (Galatians 5.22–25)

Those who make up this glorious but flawed body of Christ on earth, reflecting the multicoloured wisdom of God, can expect to be 'guided by the Spirit' (v. 25). But what might that look like in practice? In order to discern the answer to that question, many churches embark on processes to cast a vision and form a strategy to make that vision a reality, but is that what Paul is getting at here? How do the people of God 'discern' together? And what has strategy to do with the kingdom?

On the limits of a strategy

For a few strangely blissful weeks in the first lockdown of the COVID pandemic, in the spring of 2020, everything stopped.

Then we discovered Zoom and decided to Change Absolutely Everything. Why?

Several factors played into this scenario. First, all the ways in which we usually did things came to a halt. Like going into church buildings and holding services of worship – everything had to be done online. Like turning up and sitting in circles and having meetings – everything needed to happen on Zoom. Like doing school assemblies and holding synod meetings and visiting – because we couldn't.

For a while, all was zero-ed and we had little to do. But we're not very good at having nothing to do. For church leaders, who are used to running on the hamster wheel of life and ministry, coming to a compete stop was a discombobulating experience. We did not know how to simply 'stop', so we thought we'd better take the opportunity to look at some things and see if we could do them better. Added to that, as we were constantly being told by those who seemed to know and who could apparently see into the future, this hiatus presented an opportunity and if we missed it, we'd regret it.

I recall seminars with speakers who had worked in war zones who told us that, in situations like this, we need to be able to go with the flow, to adapt or perish. 'Future thinkers' told us that this was a key time and we needed to use it to reimagine the ways in which we were doing All the Things . . . or to 'pivot', the buzzword at that moment. There were workshops on how to lead in uncertain times, how to future-proof your church and how to make sure that you were ready to engage with the 'new normal', whenever that turned up and whatever it ended up looking like.

And so we began to have meetings (all on Zoom, of course) about what we wanted to change. Lots and lots of meetings. The diocese in which I was a suffragan bishop at the time engaged in a huge listening exercise and what we termed a 'vision refresh', out of which emerged four priorities, to:

- follow daily (discipleship);
- speak boldly (evangelism);
- care deeply (pastoral care and social action);
- tread gently (environmental concern).

The Church of England as a whole decided to bite the bullet and do what it has never done in its 500-year history: come up with a shared vision and strategy (I always feel that those words need to take capital letters). Both these processes yielded excellent aspirations – for the Church to be more focused, with clear sets of strategic priorities.

In the Church of England, there has since emerged a vision to be Christ-centred and Jesus-shaped, and for the Church to be simpler, humbler and bolder with three priorities, which are to be:

- a church of missionary disciples;
- younger and more diverse;
- a church where a mixed ecology of church and ministry is the norm.

Under those three headings are six further bold outcomes, which aim to:

- double the number of children and young active disciples in the Church of England by 2030;
- be a Church of England that fully represents the communities we serve, in age and diversity;
- have a parish system that is revitalized for mission, so there is a pathway for every person into an accessible and contextual expression of church;
- create 10,000 new Christian communities across the four areas of home, work and education, social and digital;
- ensure that all Christians in the Church of England are envisioned, resourced and released to live as disciples of Jesus Christ in every aspect of their lives;
- see our churches becoming communities and hubs for initial and ongoing formation.[17]

All this is good.

The goals described in the vision are bold and in line with an overall vision for the Church that aspires to fulfil Jesus' command to 'Go therefore and make disciples of all nations, baptizing them in the name of the Father and of the Son and of the Holy Spirit, and teaching them to obey everything that I have commanded you' (Matthew 28.19–20).

If we are to reverse the decline of many years and come to truly represent the amazing vision for the Church in Ephesians 3.8–10 given near the beginning of this chapter, we can't afford simply to sit around and put our feet up. As the Archbishop of York Stephen Cottrell said, introducing the vision and strategy to the Church of England's General Synod:

The historic vocation of the Church of England is to be the Church for everyone everywhere. We are the national Church. We want every person we serve to have an opportunity to encounter the transformation that a life centred on Jesus Christ can bring. We therefore need to find ways of reaching and serving people in the very diverse circumstances and contexts of our national life today – in places of leisure, workplaces and education as well as local neighbourhoods. Online as well as in person.[18]

There has been a bit of a backlash against the vision and strategy, however, not least from organizations set up to ensure that the local parish church remains the centre and focus of church life. There appears to be a view that any talk of strategy automatically means a centralized, top-down approach, in which faceless bureaucrats in Church House make all the decisions about what happens to the people and clergy of St Botolph in Little Puddle or what the church there should be doing. A recent survey of Anglican clergy reflects this view:

Strategies emerging from the national Church, such as 'Renewal and Reform' and 'Strategic Development Funding', are met with resistance from those clergy who feel that the underlying objectives (in this case the much debated concept of 'growth') do not align with their own calling and understanding of ordained ministry.[19]

Equally, in a speech to the Diocesan Synod in June 2022, the Bishop of Chelmsford, Guli Francis-Dehqani, gained a good deal of social media traction when she expressed nervousness about what all the talk of 'strategy' might mean:

> as a rule I'm not so comfortable with that kind of language which is currently widely deployed in the church. It risks, it seems to me, putting too much emphasis on our human powers – that if only we try hard enough and pull together well enough and all follow the same programme, then we can solve the problems and challenges and ensure the future survival of the church, either much as it has been in the past or preferably producing a shinier, bigger, better version. The language of vision and strategy risks ignoring the reality of frailty, brokenness, sin – all of which can be redeemed of course. But it risks missing the blessings in that which is small and vulnerable and marginal, the unexpected, the surprising. It leaves us relying heavily on our own strength instead of remembering that everything depends on our faithfulness and our reliance on God.[20]

How, though, do we reconcile these positions? On the one hand, we have the declining, anxious Church that, were it simply to sit there and do nothing at all, would cease to exist in its present form (previous comments about its eternal cosmic identity notwithstanding) in twenty years or so. On the other hand, the Bishop of Chelmsford is right, of course, that this is all about God and not ourselves, and what looks small and insignificant can be the greatest blessing, whereas large and shiny things are not always healthy, despite appearances.

These perspectives need not necessarily stand in contradiction to each other, I would argue. There is nothing wrong with planning, so long as it is planning for the right things, with the right aims and goals in mind, with the right people involved in the process. The Bible is no stranger to strategic planning. Throughout its pages, we see plans being drawn up, managed and executed. Moses, Joshua, Nehemiah drew up plans and objectives. Jesus himself spoke about the need to weigh resources and to consider carefully before setting out on a particular course of action, particularly the radical journey of being one of his followers (Luke 14.31).

It seems that it is the use of language such as 'vision and strategy' which causes the most offence and negative reactions rather than the concepts themselves. When we assume that we know what is meant by the terms 'vision' and 'strategy' – with or without capitals – we will react either positively or negatively, depending on what we perceive to be under discussion. Part of the problem, it would seem, is that some people in the Church react badly to anything they view as coming from the 'secular' world of business and management, as opposed to the theological and liturgical world of the Church. The terms 'vision' and 'strategy' would be seen to fall into the former world.

It could be that we simply misunderstand one another's language rather than one another's ideas. Rather than the question being 'Should we have strategy at all?', we may want to ask, 'What is good strategy, what is bad strategy and how do we make sure that we're doing the former, not the latter?'

'Good strategy' tends to have these three elements:

a diagnosis, a guiding policy, and a coherent action. The guiding policy specifies the approach to dealing with the obstacles called out in the diagnosis. It is like a signpost, marking the direction forward but not defining the details of the trip. Coherent actions are feasible, coordinated policies, resource commitments and actions designed to carry out a guiding policy.

Conversely a 'bad strategy' is:

a false edifice built on mistaken foundations. Bad strategy may actively avoid analysing obstacles because a leader believes that negative thoughts get in the way. Leaders may create bad strategy by mistakenly treating strategy work as an exercise in goal setting rather than problem solving.[21]

Dietrich Bonhoeffer describes the fallout suffered in the Christian community when the bad strategies of one person dominate: 'When things do not go his way, he calls the effort a failure. When his ideal picture is destroyed, he sees the community going to smash. So he becomes, first the accuser of his brethren, then an accuser of God, and finally the despairing accuser of himself.'[22]

I wonder, then, if the question needs to be changed again to 'Who does the diagnosis and using which criteria?' How do we ensure that we're solving problems, not just setting impossible goals? And who decides what the problems are?

Let's think about this another way.

In order take up my role as Bishop to the Archbishops, I moved house from Cumbria to London. I had never lived in the south-east before, let alone central London. Leaving the hills, fells and lakes of Cumbria was tough, but ever so slightly compensated for by the exciting sights and sounds of the city.

My husband and I like nothing more on our days off than to go for a walk around our new neighbourhood. We don't plan where we will go. We don't aim for anywhere. When we have a whole day of leisure ahead of us, we simply walk and see where we might get to and what we might find there. We tend to start away from the main thoroughfares and have, as a result, discovered all sorts of interesting streets full of history, beautiful architecture, cafés selling delicious food, fascinating people and places.

On one of these forays, my husband suggested that we try heading off down a particular small and unsignposted side street, having no idea where it would lead or where we would come out. 'Come on,' he said, 'it will be fun!' I said, 'But what if we get lost?' 'We can't get lost', he said. 'We don't know where we're supposed to be going, so how can we possibly get lost?'

He was right and we've had some great adventures. On other days, though, such as when I have a dentist appointment or the dog needs to go to the vet, it won't do simply to set off, walk in any direction and hope we get there. On those days, when there is a task to be done, time is limited and I have an aching tooth or a grumpy old Labrador in tow, there's a need to be very clear about where I'm going, look up directions, make sure I leave time to get there, take with me what might be necessary should a dog do what a dog does on the pavement and add in a little extra time in case.

It's a bit like that with strategy and planning in the Church. There will be times when what is needed is a more exploratory approach, when we simply wander the highways and byways of society, culture and our communities, see what opportunities present themselves and respond accordingly. At other times planning and calculation are needed. People are anxious, resources are limited and we need to come up with a plan for what we're going to do next, and after that, and after that. The Church of England's current vision and strategy is one such plan. But perhaps there needs to be room within it for churches, dioceses, parishes and people to, as it were, simply wander in the streets, get lost, turn round, retrace their steps and try something new, discovering on the way all sorts of new and different ways of doing things, meeting people they never imagined they would meet.

My contention is that we need both approaches to exist in tandem with each other – the wandering the streets approach as well as the planning the route approach.

The question is, who gets to decide what the strategic priorities for the next period should be? What is the 'guiding policy' for such decisions? Sometimes it seems as though we've taken the jigsaw puzzle and tipped all the pieces out on to the table and said, 'Right, let's rearrange it all,' but, in the meantime, we've lost the lid of the box, so we're not quite sure what the overall picture is supposed to be.

It seems to me that it's OK to have a strategy, so long as the criteria for that strategy are determined not by our own cleverness, but by the values of the kingdom of God, 'the place where the will of God will be perfectly done'.[23] What might it look like to have a strategy guided by the ways of the kingdom of God?

Why strategy doesn't work 'under occupation'

First, we recognize that the ways of the kingdom are not the ways of the world. Jesus himself made that clear: 'My kingdom is not from this world' (John 18.36). The kingdom of God – that overarching framework by means of which Jesus understood his mission and we continue to view what the work of the Church is – sets itself over and against the 'kingdoms' (and powers and principalities) that occupy this world, in 'this present darkness'. We are citizens of another kingdom, living in a land under occupation, and that demands a different approach.

Ugandan theologian Emmanuel Katongole distinguishes between 'strategy' and 'tactics':

Strategy is the posture of the powerful. It sets goals and commits to measurable outcomes. It is not comfortable with uncertainties, but always accounts for them as predictable variables. On the other hand, tactics are the tools of the weak . . . Tactics are the wisdom of the weak about how to survive in a world they do not own . . . Tactics depend on the art of improvisation. When situations change, tactics change with them.[24]

Katongole holds that using tactics is the way Jesus trained his disciples to operate, in a kind of 'guerrilla war' against the powers and principalities of this world. Jesus did not present a well worked-out strategy but, instead, taught his disciples tactics for 'subverting the dominant economic order and creating new possibilities within it',[25] such as turn the other cheek, forgive debts, settle matters quickly. Did Jesus have a strategy? He certainly seemed to know why he had come, his 'guiding policy' that he set out plainly at the beginning of his ministry:

The Spirit of the Lord is upon me,
   because he has anointed me
      to bring good news to the poor.
He has sent me to proclaim release to
      the captives
   and recovery of sight to the blind,
      to let the oppressed go free,
to proclaim the year of the Lord's
      favour.
(Luke 4.18–19)[26]

Yet, day by day, he was responsive to the people he met and told his disciples, 'Very truly, I tell you, the Son can do nothing on his own, but only what he sees the Father doing; for whatever the Father does, the Son does likewise' (John 5.19). He didn't lay out the strategy before them in a step-by-step fashion, but gave them the 'tactics', the 'signposts' they needed, mostly by telling them stories to help them to understand the plans and purposes of God's kingdom. Most of the stories left them bemused, however, as they tried to work out what he was on about.

Business leaders speak of the need for 'complex adaptive systems' that can flex and flow in response to change – in a way more akin to the murmuration of a flock of birds than a linear flow chart. In these complex times, ultimately, any strategic planning that does not allow for complexity and constant change will fall short. A series of events, including the COVID pandemic, the war in Ukraine and resulting cost of living crisis, plus, in the UK, the fallout following Brexit, means we can no longer make predictions about the future with the same kind of certainty that we once did.

Margaret Heffernan sums up the situation: 'We have moved from a complicated world to a complex one. The two aren't the same – and complexity isn't just complicated on steroids.'[27] In terms of strategic planning, the complicated and the complex need to be approached differently. Complicated environments are linear and can be planned for and with some predictability. In complex environments, however, even small shifts can have major impacts that necessitate a radical re-evaluation of all our plans. Planning during times of complexity requires a whole new way of thinking and working, a completely different set of skills. Heffernan suggests:

> We can't acquire these skills until we accept uncertainty and start to do the extra work needed to produce communities, companies and countries that are robust. Not merely efficient. Not simply rich. But able to withstand shocks we cannot see coming. That means we all need to get good at change. At convening. At listening. At seeing each other as a source of strength.[28]

I wonder what this says to the Church? What is needed in a time of flux is stability and kindness. Perhaps *what* we do matters much less than *how* we do it.

Why we don't 'build the kingdom'

Second, when our strategies are determined by the kingdom of God, we will recognize that their success or otherwise does not depend on our own effort – far from it. We need to learn to see, and therefore act, through the lens of the kingdom of God, which is a reality and a gift.

What do I mean by that? I have long had an issue with people (or songs) that speak of us 'building God's kingdom'. Here, there or anywhere. The kingdom of God is that present yet provisional reality inaugurated by the life, ministry, death and resurrection of Christ, but which will not come in full until the end of time, when God returns to reign on the earth and every tear will be dried and the ways and works of God will be seen everywhere. Until that day, we live in this provisional space, waiting, watching and seeing glimpses of the kingdom when it breaks through from the future into the present.

There is, indeed, a need to live *in* the kingdom. Jesus tells us to seek the kingdom (Matthew 6.33), to enter the kingdom (19.24), to inherit the kingdom (25.34), to receive the kingdom (Mark 10.15), to wait expectantly for the kingdom (15.43), to proclaim the kingdom (Luke 9.2) and to testify to the kingdom (Acts 28.23). We can herald it and point to it and live in the light of it, but the one thing we *can't* do with the kingdom is build it. Only God can do that. It is a reality beyond ourselves and does not depend on us. Though we cannot build the kingdom, we can build *for* the kingdom. Maybe this fact is to prevent us from becoming too obsessed with our own plans.

The best description of strategy I have heard came from the Archbishop of Kenya, Jackson Ole Sapit. I once had the pleasure of being stuck in a very long Nairobi traffic jam with him. What was supposed to be a short journey from the hotel where we were staying to a place we were visiting took hours. It was at a time when my own diocese in England was exploring the possibility of church planting. I knew that those in the Anglican Church of Kenya had experienced phenomenal growth through church planting and I wanted to know how they had gone about it. 'This', I thought, 'is my opportunity to ask him lots of questions about his strategy – how they had planned the church plants, how they had resourced them, trained the leaders, monitored outcomes, assessed effectiveness.'

I started, 'Archbishop, I would like to ask you about your strategy for church planting. Please could you explain it to me?' He looked at me and smiled. 'We read what it says in the Bible and we do it', he said.

Why a strategy must include failure

Third, a kingdom-orientated strategy will leave plenty of room for failure. Joe Moran writes, 'We should learn to live with failure for a little while. It might make us think about what success really amounts to, and why it's rarely the answer to our problems we mistook it for.'[29]

We noted in Chapter 2 how fear of failure is one of the greatest hindrances to the kind of exploratory testing and experimentation that is necessary to expand knowledge and investigate new possibilities. This is no less true in the Church, especially when we are seeking to try something new, as is the case with the stated aim to start 10,000 new church plants.

Organizations, and churches, that wish to try new things cannot be hampered by a fear of failure and must learn to take appropriate risks. Church numbers are not looking good and we need to do something about that. However, our anxiety about reversing the decline of the Church can lead to an obsession with growth and a short-termism that does not allow sufficient time and space to make mistakes.

The courage to risk failure in order to try new things is a particular quality needed at present in our church leaders. In 2016, the Faith and Order Commission's report on senior leadership in *Faithful Improvisation?* suggested that:

as we pursue diverse improvisations in leadership, we must not mistake failure for disaster. Some improvisations will fail – or, at least, they will not produce the renewal or the growth or the depth that we hoped for. Sometimes, there may be lessons that our prayerful reflection can learn from such failures; often, even with the benefit of hindsight, it will be hard to see what else could have been done . . . We therefore have to cultivate a culture that allows failure, that attends to it carefully and learns from it seriously, but that does not condemn it. In part, this is because we will certainly not encourage real improvisation and experimentation if we have generated an atmosphere of performance anxiety; improvisation is only made possible by trust.[30]

Without embracing the reality of failure in our plans and strategies, we are likely to becomes obsessed with goal-setting, to aim for misguided ideas of what success looks like and to miss the opportunities for risk and innovation that come bundled up with the possibility of failure. It is notoriously difficult, however, for us to judge what success means in a church context and, therefore, what failure looks like also.

Perhaps the challenge when we are trying new things is to decide what kind of failure is acceptable. Some failures waste other people's money. Some failures cause hurt and damage. Some failures set back the cause of the gospel for generations. So how do we decide what failure is acceptable as we work out our strategy? How do we try to fail well when trying new things in the Church? By what criteria do we measure success and, therefore, failure? How do we recognize a failing church? Does such a term even make sense anyway?

I have written elsewhere about the strengths and weaknesses of numbers as a means of measuring growth in the Church.[31] We need to admit that numbers are too blunt an instrument for the kinds of small and fragile growth we might expect and look for when God begins to birth something new in uncertain times. One church planter who experienced the reality of failure in his attempts to start a new worshipping community laments that our obsession with numbers makes assessing success (and, therefore, failure) in a church context very difficult:

> We so easily get drawn into similar models of success as businesses, social enterprises or schools. We look for things that can be measured or counted. In church this means we look for numbers. It can be numbers of people there on a Sunday, numbers of friends or followers on social media, numbers in the evangelism course or at the event last week.[32]

Paul Bradbury points out the predominance of 'left-brain domination' in our thinking about what constitutes success or failure in the Church, describing this as 'a hall of mirrors where it struggles to see beyond particular formularies and structures of church, and a particular means of measuring them'. Rather than measuring everything (worse still, counting everything), Bradbury advocates that we begin to also *evaluate* the new thing we are involved with, evaluation being 'making sense of what God is doing' and, thus, involving 'the process of revealing its secrets, unveiling its nature'.[33]

When I was a bishop in Cumbria, a lot of our diocesan strategy involved the encouragement of pioneering and innovation in a church context. Permission (and funds) were given to the starting of new worshipping communities, many of them among young people. The grant-making bodies within the Church that gave the funds enabling such innovations understandably required that the money be accounted for and expected an effective return on their investment.

Annual reports had to be submitted that involved the counting and measuring of things: how many people had joined the new churches, how many baptisms there had been, what the financial sustainability of the initiative was looking like. That is all well and good and we understood the need to give a realistic account of what was happening, but, increasingly, we began to feel uncomfortable about the criteria for measurement being requested. Yes, new people had joined the churches, but had they grown in discipleship at all? And what does it mean to 'join' a church anyway? How long do you have to be there to count as a member? And how on earth do you measure 'new Christians'? At what point do you determine that someone has 'become a Christian'? There's no exam to take or test to pass.

Providing numbers for all these things seemed to be extremely problematic. We began to experiment instead with the idea of evaluating how people had grown or developed in their faith, whether they were starting 'while they were still far off' or whether they'd been disciples all their lives and their faith had grown, developed and matured. We determined that no one else can say these things for you. Only individuals can say for themselves if they have become a Christian or have grown or matured in their faith. So we began to develop a means whereby, in the context of prayer and worship, people could, year on year, assess for themselves whether or not and how they had changed, or been changed, in the previous year; if they considered that they'd grown closer to God, they'd prayed more, read their Bible more or with greater understanding or differently, if they'd become more engaged with their local community, loved their neighbour better, become more confident about speaking about their faith with others. We tried to evaluate in terms of faithfulness and fruitfulness, not efficiency and effectiveness, because 'our lives and ministries will be assessed by congruence, not efficiency. It is not found in productivity, competence or progress as much as in the development of Christlike character and coherence of our stories with the character of God.'[34] According to these criteria, no one, no church, no leader, no minister, no congregation member and no initiative would ever be deemed a failure. Pope Francis once expressed this in a homily to his priests:

We can get caught up measuring the value of our apostolic works by the standards of efficiency, good management, and outward success which govern the business world. Not that these things are unimportant!

We have been entrusted with a great responsibility, and God's people rightly expect accountability from us. But the true worth of our apostolate is measured by the value it has in God's eyes. To see and evaluate things from God's perspective calls for constant conversion in the first days and years of our vocation and, need I say, it calls for great humility. The cross shows us a different way of measuring success. Ours is to plant the seeds: God sees to the fruits of our labors. And if at times our efforts and works seem to fail and produce no fruit, we need to remember that we are followers of Jesus . . . and his life, humanly speaking, ended in failure, in the failure of the cross.[35]

Conclusion: the grammar of the Church

At the beginning of this chapter, I tried (and probably failed) to set out a vision for who and what the Church is – a high and cosmic picture that exists as a sign and sacrament of reconciliation to demonstrate the very wisdom of God in our fractured and broken world. I have also shown (probably also unsuccessfully) some of the ways in which the Church fails to live up to those ideals. Daily. So how should we think of the Church now?

I am a linguist by background and (here is my confession), I love grammar. I will happily yell at the TV until I am blue in the face if a presenter fails to use 'few' and 'less' correctly. I go apoplectic over a split infinitive. I have put my grammatical pedantry to good use, however, and I have begun to think in grammatical terms about the Church.

The Church is a slippery entity. Understanding it fully is like trying to get an octopus into a string bag – just when you think that you've got all the legs in, another one pops out and you have to start again. Similarly, as soon as I think that I have worked out what or who the Church is and is supposed to be, she does and says something different that demonstrates the opposite. It was no surprise to me that one of the most difficult parts of the Living in Love and Faith process has been any attempt to try to define and understand an adequate ecclesiology (long word for 'what is the Church?') for it. So, let's try something with grammar. What might it look like to think of the Church according to different grammatical terms?

We tend to think most often of 'church' as a noun – an 'object' word. Indeed, that is what it is, technically, as a part of speech: 'church'. But the problem with seeing it as a noun is that we see it as immutable, unmoving, a Thing. And when we see church as a Thing, we tend to fall into the trap of adding various descriptive adjectives and delineating this kind of Thing from that kind of Thing. So we find ourselves describing different *kinds* of church – traditional church, fresh expressions of church, resource church, resourcing church (subtly different), ordinary parish church – and, depending on our preferences, setting up barriers between them and pitting one against another in competitions for attention, priorities and resources.

When I arrived in Cumbria, one of the things that struck me first was the division that existed between different 'kinds' of church. Recent growth in 'fresh expressions' of church tended to be set over and against so-called 'traditional church'. I found these terms value-laden and problematic. What is the opposite of 'fresh expressions of church' anyway? Stale church? 'Traditional' tended be equated with unmoving and boring.

We began to use the term 'time-honoured' church instead. One of the things that I tended to say a lot in my early days in the role was 'It's all church', but the problem is, it's not, is it? At least not in our heads, and when we say 'church', we tend to assume, wrongly, that everyone will know what is meant by that and will be imagining the same thing. So 'church' as a noun causes problems. Paul Bradbury says:

> We hear the word as if all the context and narrative contained within any expression of Christian community has been stripped out and boiled down into some generic image, probably a pew-stuffed building with a dot-matrix congregation awaiting a venerable cleric.[36]

James Rebanks in his book *English Pastoral* makes an equivalent point about farming. There is a trend at the moment to 'rewild' everything and Rebanks describes how, on his farm, he has tried to reverse the more destructive farming methods of the past intended purely to increase crop yields but without much care for the authenticity, sustainability and diversity of the natural landscape:

> I want a farm full of birdsong, insects, animals and beautiful plants and trees. It should run

overwhelmingly on sunlight not fossil fuels. We are shifting to using fewer drugs and chemicals, and less bought-in feed. We use almost no pesticides and I hope it soon can be none.[37]

Yet, he has also come to the view that the process of rewilding itself can be a damaging obsession, and both older *and* newer methods are needed for a farm to be truly effective:

The idea that land must be either perfectly wild or perfectly efficient and sterile is unwise and blinding; it is false and unsustainable simplification. When we despair and reduce our world view to black and white – 'farming' is bad; 'nature' is good – we lose sight of vital distinctions and nuances. We make every farmer who isn't a saint a villain. We miss the actual complexities of farming, the vast spectrum between these two extremes and the massive scope for nature-friendly farming that exists between them.[38]

I wonder what that paragraph sounds like if we substitute 'old ways of doing church' for 'farming' and 'new innovations and fresh expressions' for 'nature'?

There is a rich vein of thinking in the Church that calls for its rewilding, in a similar way to the rewilding of the landscape,[39] yet we should remember that we need both the old and the new, the established and the fresh, tradition and innovation.

How about 'church' as a verb – a 'doing' word? I first came across Godfrey Rust's poem 'Church is a verb' at a retreat several years ago. It's a marvellous poem that speaks of all that the Church does, and is, and ends with the lines: 'There will come a time for church to get dressed up ready for its marriage, ready to settle down and become a noun – but until then church is the living Word spoken in verbs.'[40]

But 'church' as a verb doesn't always work terribly well either. It has associations with the now defunct service of the 'churching of women' after childbirth or the awful verbs to 'dechurch' or 'rechurch' someone. Additionally, if 'church' as a noun is about being, then 'church' as a verb is about doing, and could lead us to imagine that our activism will lead us out of our current crisis. As the Archbishop of Canterbury said in one of his keynote addresses to the Lambeth Conference in 2022:

> A key mark of declining institutions or companies or countries – and churches – is that they may have a vision of what they should do, they may even have a clear strategy: they just can't turn their strategy into action. There is no implementing of the strategy. So the question is not always 'what should we do?' We do need to ask that question. Archbishop Stephen answered that: we worship, and we make disciples. We know what we should do. But the problem is how?[41]

So let's think about the 'how', let's try 'church' as an adjective or adverb – a describing word.

As this chapter has explored, I believe that we need to focus less on what we are, and the limits and boundaries of that, less on what we do, and the way our own efforts might save us, and more on the way we are together, the quality of our being and our relating – *how* we are church.

The Church is made up of a whole load of failures – imperfect saints in various times and places who constantly mess up, get it wrong, wound one another and the world around us, fail to say 'Sorry' properly, pitch one part against another, lose our way. Let's be kind to one another and focus more on the descriptive qualities that have the potential to bring us together, not drive us apart – kind church, loving church, patient church, joyful church, bold church.

For, in the end, we are, together, a demonstration of the wisdom of God – no more and no less. As the Church, that's what we have to offer. We're not second-rate politicians or rubbish social workers. The answer to all our crises is not to come up with more clever plans but preach Christ crucified. We're not to be disappointed idealists but optimistic realists, and we will sensibly improvise our way into God's future.

Above all, we have a hope based on the immutable fact that Jesus Christ lived, died and rose again, and left on earth a people – his bride (the Church) – to work with him, in the power of his Spirit, to reveal glimpses of his kingdom on earth, so that when he returns, he will recognize us – a simpler, bolder, humbler church of missional disciples. At the end of *English Pastoral*, Rebanks says this about farming – again, his words may apply equally to the Church:

> There are a million reasons to believe that we are not big enough, brave enough or wise enough to do anything so grand and idealistic as stop the damage we are doing . . . The world of human beings is ugly, selfish and mean, and we are easily misled and divided. And yet, despite everything, I believe we, you and I, each in our own ways, can do the things that are necessary.[42]

Amen, Mr Shepherd. Amen.

For discussion

1 How do you honestly feel about the Church?
2 How central to your understanding of the gospel is the concept of the spiritual unity of the body of Christ?
3 What is your personal response to the sins Paul lists in Galatians 5 in the context of church life? Where do you see room for hope?

5

The greatest failure of all

LEE: . . . There's no doubt. Only the certainty of being
saved.
DAVID: That must be very comforting.
LEE: It is. I don't know why you don't try it.
DAVID: I don't try it because life isn't like that. It's
nuanced. You, of all people should understand that,
Lee. It's a mess.
S. Beresford, *The Southbury Child* (2022)

Jesus spent a lot of time with failures. So much so, it was
the thing that got him into trouble most often with the
religious authorities (Matthew 9.10–11; Luke 5:29–30;
19.5–7). The way Jesus responded to people whom society
deemed to have failed in some way or another (including
tax collectors and prostitutes) was to eat with them, to
spend time with them, to call them his friends. He did
not wait for failures to become respectable or 'successful'
before he welcomed them into the kingdom. Indeed, he
said to the supposedly righteous chief priests and elders,
'Truly I tell you, the tax-collectors and the prostitutes are
going into the kingdom of God ahead of you' (Matthew
21.31). The thing that got Jesus crucified – among all the
various things that really angered the religious leaders
and occupying forces – was his claim to forgive sins. It

put him on a par with God, which, of course, was exactly the point.

So, Jesus had a lot of time for failures.

Setting them up to fail

Jesus also trained his disciples for failure. He seemed to do it a lot. He did that rather than give them the kind of motivational training session we might associate with the residential leadership training new recruits are given these days. Jesus knew that the path to which he had called them was strewn with difficulties and more likely to earn them suffering than success, grief rather than glory. He challenged them to drink the same cup of suffering that he did (Matthew 20.22) and even prepared them for their deaths (Matthew 16.25). He sent them out in the sure knowledge that they would encounter rejection more often than recognition.

Kenneth Bailey asserts that, essentially, Jesus' sending out of the Twelve (Mark 6.10–11) is a 'theology of failure'. Jesus trains his disciples in what to do when (not if) they encounter failure as they bring the good news of the kingdom to those they meet:

> Wherever you enter a house, stay there until you leave the place. If any place will not welcome you and they refuse to hear you, as you leave, shake off the dust that is on your feet as a testimony against them.
> (Mark 6.10–11)

'Shaking off the dust', Bailey says:

is a symbolic gesture that means 'I am finished with you and am leaving. Furthermore, as I leave, I take nothing from this house, not even its dust' (Acts 13:51, 18:6). This dramatic gesture can help the apostles leave behind them any lingering sense of failure. It frees them to go on (like Paul and his band) to the next home or village 'filled with joy and the Holy Spirit' (Acts 13:52). Having tried and failed, they must move on. It is astounding to see Jesus on this very first outreach beyond the range of his voice offering advice on how to deal with failure.[1]

Jesus does likewise when sending out the seventy in Luke 10, adding on that occasion, 'Whoever listens to you listens to me, and whoever rejects you rejects me, and whoever rejects me rejects the one who sent me' (v. 16).

We see Jesus teaching his disciples about failure again in Matthew 17, when a sick boy's father comes to him and says, 'I brought him to your disciples, but they could not cure him' (v. 16). His disciples, understandably, are bothered by their failure to do what Jesus had been teaching them to do, and they ask him why they could not manage it. Jesus seems both to name the reality of the situation ('Because of your little faith', v. 20) and also offer hope that things could be different ('if you have faith the size of a mustard seed, you will say to this mountain, "Move from here to there", and it will move; and nothing will be impossible for you', v. 20). That is what Jesus does again and again with the failures of his disciples. He names the reality of the situation and offers another, hopeful, chance to try again. And again. That's what he does with Peter, Mary, James and John, Zacchaeus, Thomas, the woman at the well. Everyone.

One of the most compelling and enigmatic stories in the Gospels depicts Jesus' encounter with a failure. We meet a woman whose search for love has got her into a great deal of trouble in John, chapter 8. As the woman stands in the dust, guilty as charged (John leaves us in no doubt about that – she had been 'caught in the very act of committing adultery', v. 4), the scribes and the Pharisees (elsewhere condemned by Jesus for not recognizing their own sinfulness) challenge Jesus to remember the rules and the law of Moses, that she should be stoned to death. 'Now what do you say?' they demand. No mention of the man involved, incidentally, but then they don't really want to resolve the situation – the woman is simply a pawn in their game to try to catch Jesus out. It's a trap, of course: if he says she shouldn't be stoned, he's defying the law of Moses (Leviticus 20.10); if he says she should, he's breaking the rules of the Roman rulers. He can't win. Keeping *all* the rules is an impossibility. They're setting him up for failure.

As the woman stands before him, Jesus speaks neither to her nor to the scribes and Pharisees. He bends down and writes in the dust.

Writes what? Isn't it ever so frustrating that we are not told? Haven't you wondered? What did he write? Some of the rules maybe? Leviticus 20, verse 10? An instruction to the woman? Her name? Maybe he just doodled, playing for time. Here he is, bending down, lowering himself, identifying with her in her low state. All the accusers standing round, peering down at him. They must have been wondering too, thinking, 'What on earth is he doing?'

Whatever it was, he then straightens up and speaks – still not to the woman but to her accusers: 'Let anyone among you who is without sin be the first to throw a stone at her' (John 8.7). As my kids would say, 'Awkward.'

Cleverly, in this way Jesus invites them to examine themselves, not the woman, and to see if they, too, are failures. Knowing that this particular rule disqualifies them all, they begin to slope away, one by one, until two are left. Jesus and the woman. Alone.

It's a poignant and provocative scene. Augustine describes it with a Latin play on words: *relicti sunt duo, misera et misericordia* ('two were left, misery and mercy'). Then, only then, once those who condemned the woman have dispersed, Jesus looks her in the eye and says, 'Go your way, and . . . do not sin again' (John 8.11). Here we have a picture of what failure looks like to Jesus, looking up at us from the dust.

Jesus was used to dealing with failure in others. He anticipated the failure of his disciples, trained them for it even, and was merciful when he encountered failure in those he met, always giving them a second chance. So, here's the big question: did Jesus himself ever fail?

'You've never failed'

As I write this, I have just returned from a service of worship in which we sang a popular Christian song. It's very familiar, one of those 'go-to' worship songs. It's a lovely one, all about God's faithfulness and support in troubled and stormy times. And it has a banging tune. Today, though, as we sang, I was caught out by my reaction to a few lines that I hadn't really noticed before, presumably about Jesus, declaring that, when we are beset by fear, 'You've never failed'.[2]

Now, I know what the songwriters were trying to express here and I appreciate the sentiment. These are words of trust in God, that he will uphold me in times of fear and uncertainty and he won't fail *at that particular task*, but it was the phrase 'You've never failed' that stood out to me starkly as never before.

The whole premise of this book is that failure is an intrinsic part of everyday human experience, not something to be fearful of, embarrassed about or ashamed of, but owned, confronted and learned from. Additionally, for many people, myself included, an important dimension of faith in Jesus Christ is the Incarnation – the knowledge that, in becoming human, Jesus entered into human experience, lived as one of us and, therefore, is able to identify with all our human desires, struggles and vulnerabilities, in all respects. Except one, apparently: 'You've never failed.'

According to the song, in this one, central, crucial, everyday aspect of our human experience – the experience of failure – Jesus is unable to empathize with us because he has never failed. Not only has he never failed but he's not about to start.

I know, I know, the song is really about God and not Jesus, specifically. I know that what the song says is not so different from what is expressed in Hebrews 4.15: 'For we do not have a high priest who is unable to sympathize with our weaknesses, but we have one who in every respect has been tested as we are, yet without sin.' But the song doesn't say 'without sin', it says 'never failed'.

As we examine this significant human experience – failure – can Jesus identify with us in our weakness? Is failure part of the human experience that Jesus, who came to redeem our humanity, himself experienced? How important is it that Jesus 'suffered as we do, yet without sin'? Russ Parker writes, 'failure is written into the heart of the gospel, for the one who is the good news himself faced limitations and failure'.[3]

Did he? Did Jesus ever know failure?

There are many ways in which Jesus' ministry would be judged as unsuccessful by those looking on, including us from the perspective of more than 2,000 intervening years of history. He was rejected when he tried to preach in his home town, and so offended the people there with his message, that they tried to throw him off a cliff (Luke 4.20–30). His own family thought that he'd gone mad (Mark 3.21). He constantly failed to convince his closest followers of his intent and purpose (Matthew 16.22–23). The religious leaders conspired to kill him (Matthew 26.3–4). In the end, he was deserted by all but a few of his closest friends and his mother (John 19.25–27). He died an ignominious death (Matthew 27.35–56). He never had a home (Matthew 8.20) and, when he died, he was laid in a borrowed tomb (Luke 23.50–54).

Earlier, in Chapter 2, we alighted on a simple definition of failure as 'when things don't go according to plan'. How could Jesus have failed when he was perfect? As a human being, though, he was not immune to failure – at least, failure in human terms, according to the plans and purposes of others, not the plans and purposes of God. 'Whatever the Father does, the Son does likewise', he said (John 5.19).

Perhaps with Jesus we need to turn again to the grammar of failure. Jesus was without sin, so he could not make mistakes. He was never in error. He was not A Failure, ultimately, although he did *experience* failure. In the earliest Church, there was a Gnostic view that Jesus could not really have entered into bodily experiences. He only looked as though he ate and drank and laughed and cried and so on, but he didn't really. He existed, rather, in a state of 'divine impassibility', only *appearing* to experience human emotion. That, though, is a heresy because it denies the full, bodily humanity of Jesus. He was hungry, tired and sometimes, it seems, irritable. He lived a full range of bodily and emotional states, but without sinning. Failure is not a sin. And the fact that Jesus experienced failure means that he has sanctified the experience for us.

The parable of the sower: a message about failure

Even if you reject Jesus as the Son of God and all the miracles stuff, surely his teaching is what is most successful, isn't it? Again, it depends what you mean by successful. If success means that everyone who heard his message turned to God, repented, followed him and began to live in the ways of the kingdom, then, no, Jesus' message was not a complete success. It wasn't then and it isn't now. In fact, Jesus himself told a story to illustrate what a failure his own preaching was.

The parable of the sower in Matthew 13 should be a great encouragement to preachers everywhere. We often gloss over the real intent of Jesus in telling this parable, not helped by the fact that, when the parable is listed in the lectionary, half its context – the part explaining the message Jesus was trying to convey – is missed out.

Jesus tells a story that illustrates what proclaiming the message of the kingdom is like, but he also goes on to explain the story to his disciples. It's a story about those who think that they have heard, but have not heard, and those who hear, but don't understand. Just before he tells the story, we read about Jesus' conflicts with the Pharisees, who are plotting to destroy him (Matthew 12.14). Jesus is at odds with his own family (12.46–50) and, by the end of chapter 13, his home town will have taken offence too (vv. 54–58). To say that his message got a mixed reception is to put it mildly, and his teaching in this parable goes some way to explaining why.

It's a parable about what happens when the message of the kingdom is sown, then accepted or rejected. His followers were expecting revolution. All this talk of the kingdom led them to hope for a powerful overthrowing of the Roman occupiers and restoration of the nation of Israel, but Jesus' kingdom comes about not by force, but by telling people about it. It is the word, not the sword that announces his kingdom. It's a gentle, peaceful revolution, brought about by words and by death, so Jesus told them a story that begins, 'A sower went out to sow . . .' (Matthew 13.3).

As we know well, four things happened to the seeds: some fell on the path and the birds came and ate them up; some fell on rocky ground, seedlings sprang up, were scorched by the sun and withered; some fell among thorns, which grew and choked them; others fell on good soil and produced grain. Nice story, but what does it mean?

Good question. 'Why do you teach in parables?', the disciples asked. In answering them, Jesus quotes Isaiah 6.9–10: 'You will indeed listen, but never understand, and you will indeed look, but never perceive. For this people's heart has grown dull, and their ears are hard of hearing, and they have shut their eyes.' Only those who have the eyes and ears of faith, who choose to follow Jesus, who are ready to receive his truth, will be able truly to understand the meaning of the story, he says. This is a hard teaching.

The parable is about the challenge, unacceptability, inaccessibility, hiddenness of the message of the gospel, which can't be understood from the outside, but depends on revelation to comprehend the mystery. Access to the kingdom is not easy and cheap. It must be wrestled with, puzzled over and understood – or not.

In the end, Jesus says, only about a quarter of the seed of the word of the gospel that is sown will bear good fruit for the kingdom. The parable of the sower reminds us that preaching, scattering the word of the kingdom, has always been hard work with few guaranteed results. It's a sobering reminder that even Jesus expected only about 25 per cent of his words to bear real fruit. With the obsession in today's Church with results and effectiveness, Jesus' depiction of the apparent ineffectiveness of his own ministry may serve to lend us some encouragement.

The parable also reminds us that we are to be faithful in spreading the word widely and abundantly, but the result may be a failure, as it was for Jesus. We are to be generous and fling words around in even the least promising places, but leave the outcome to God. William Willimon puts it like this in relation to preaching:

> Though failure is expected, our job as preachers is Sunday-upon-Sunday to sling the seed; the harvest is up to God. Preachers don't work alone. It's not a sermon until the Holy Spirit shows up, rips a sermon out of my hands, makes a dull religious lecture into pyrotechnic proclamation, and enables my words to cavort through the exposed congregation. Like I said, if anybody hears, it's a miracle.[4]

So if Jesus' understanding of his own mission allowed room for failure, what about the end-point of that ministry, his death on a cross? Surely that constitutes the ultimate failure?

The 'failure' of the cross?

I recall vividly the time when I went before a selection panel to help me to discern whether or not God was calling me to train to be an ordained minister in the Church of England. I was 25 at the time and mother to a small baby. Interviews were held to assess my pastoral, educational and spiritual fitness for theological study and ordained ministry. I was exhausted and when all the candidates went to the pub on the first evening, as was expected ('Yes! Here I am! A sociable person!'), I longed simply to go to bed and catch up on much needed sleep. Through the fog of my baby brain I am surprised now that I could even remember my own name, yet somehow I managed (apparently adequately, since I was indeed recommended to train for ordination) to answer the probing questions of the interviewers.

Among the panoply of questions and group exercises (terrifying) and psychometric tests ('Is that ink blot supposed to be a butterfly or a rabbit? If I get it wrong, will they think I'm mad?'), I vividly recall two particular questions. One was this: 'You smile a lot. What's behind that smile?' Goodness, I can't even remember how I answered that one. The second was: 'In what sense, if any, do you recognize the failure of God?' I know! You have a go!

The interviewer knew from my paperwork that I had a fairly conservative background and I suspect he thought such matters were not often talked about, so I think he was trying to test me and, possibly, catch me out. Was my view of God really all rosiness and sunflowers? Did I have any room in my shiny theology for a suffering God?

Inside, I was all of a dither and spent the rest of the interview after that question thinking that I had truly mucked up and ruined my chances. I do remember, though, that my bumbling response was something about the cross and, on the cross, maybe Jesus thought he had failed. And Jesus was God. So maybe God did fail. A little bit. For a while. And so perhaps that means he knows what we feel like when we fail. As we all do. Is that OK, and please can I be a vicar?

When we speak of Jesus and failure, inevitably we end up at the cross. Much writing about failure also ends up there, and rightly so, but much of it is about how the cross *seemed* to be failure when, actually, it is the pathway to success. After crucifixion comes resurrection. It's Friday, but Sunday's coming. Hence, John Navone writes:

> The cross raised the question of failure which the resurrection answered. God *seemed* to have failed Jesus. Jesus *felt* forsaken and was taunted by those who told him to come down from the cross if he was truly the son of God. Jesus *seemed* to have failed his father in not having converted Israel. Israel had *apparently* failed its God by not having accepted Jesus, his word.[5]
> (Italics mine)

The key words here are 'felt', 'seemed' and 'apparently'. The cross wasn't *really* a failure – the resurrection proves that. Parker gets a bit closer to acknowledging that there is, in the cross, a hint that failure is not a once-and-for-all experience leading to great success, but a daily calling to potential suffering:

So it is that Jesus calls us to take up our cross and follow him. In doing so, he reminds us that the cross is not some temporary spiritual dark night of the soul which, once endured, leads us on into better times of success and maturity; the cross is a continuous experience of living with suffering and failure.[6]

But that is more about the experience of discipleship, which involves a daily taking up of the cross, rather than making any claim about the 'failure' of the cross.

I am in no doubt that the cross felt like failure to Jesus. That's why he cried out, 'My God, my God, why have you forsaken me?' (Matthew 27.46; Mark 15.34). In this way we can say that Jesus *experienced* failure as we do. He experienced desolation. Yet, the cross was very much not failure. If failure is when something doesn't go to plan, the cross was not failure because the cross was God's plan all along – and Jesus knew that and taught his disciples as much: 'The Son of Man must undergo great suffering, and be rejected by the elders, chief priests, and scribes, and be killed, and on the third day be raised' (Luke 9.22).

What felt like failure to Jesus, then, was not the lack of things progressing according to the plan, but his experience of complete separation from God, being forsaken. The death of Christ on the cross involved physical suffering, for sure, but more than that, it involved spiritual suffering. As Calvin puts it, his suffering was beyond physical: 'not only was the body of Christ given up as the price of redemption but . . . there was a greater and more excellent price – that he bore in his soul in the tortures of condemned and ruined man'.[7]

On the cross, Jesus Christ experienced the ultimate failure – the separation of the Godhead, as 'For our sake he made him to be sin who knew no sin, so that in him we might become the righteousness of God' (2 Corinthians 5.21). We will never, ever experience the same kind of failure that Jesus experienced on the cross, precisely because he was Christ and we are not. We will not experience separation from God because we are not the Messiah. We will also never experience separation from God precisely *because of* the cross. Because of the suffering Jesus experienced there, we will never be distant from God, no matter how bad our failure. There is always hope, always redemption – because of the cross, the ultimate symbol of failure.

So I will be bold and say that I don't think the cross is the place to go if we are seeking comfort for our own failures. In my answer to my selection panel interrogator – sorry, 'selector' – I was right to say that the cross *seemed* like failure. But it only seemed like it. It wasn't really. I don't think that there is any sense at all in which God has failed. Ever. *You've never failed.* That is the truth which means he is able to deal with all my failure, because he has never, ever failed. Of course the cross is the answer to all our failures, for, in the cross, Jesus overcame sin and death and hell and all the sin and failure that exists in our world and our hearts, which means, ultimately, the end of all failure for everyone.

Jesus was God and we're not, so he never knew the failure we experience, including the ultimate 'failure' that is dying and staying dead. Easter Sunday and the resurrection show us that failure is never final and what often looks like failure turns out to be an incredible success. In the light of this success, we see all our failures. That's all well and good, but how does this enable us to live with what we experience day by day as ultimate failure? When it's a rainy Tuesday and your life seems full of failure, is that the comfort you need? The cross seemed like failure but, actually, it was the most rip-roaring success?

There was a day where no one knew whether the cross was successful or not – when Jesus' body lay in a tomb. Between Good Friday and Easter Sunday is a day that sings of failure.

It's called Holy Saturday.

The longest Saturday

My family spent several years as part of the Lee Abbey community in north Devon. It was a wonderful time in our lives, when our children were young and we lived with a residential community of nearly 100 mostly young people, welcoming a variety of guests each year for retreats, conferences and house parties. One of the most popular holiday weeks was over Easter. The resident community would spend a great deal of time and effort preparing, rehearsing for and presenting a Passion play – a retelling of the Easter story, with a different scene taking place each day through the week-long retreat, different members of the community playing the key parts of the Passion narrative. The various events of Holy Week and Easter were enacted on the relevant days of Holy Week, around the incredibly beautiful 300-acre estate. On Maundy Thursday, we gathered for a shared meal and foot-washing. On Good Friday, we walked up the hill above the house, sat on the grass and wept as someone playing Jesus was 'crucified' in as realistic a manner as we could muster. On Easter Sunday, very early, we followed some of the community women playing Mary and the other disciples to a small grotto carved into the rock face of one of the cliffs near the seashore. There we would marvel at the abandoned grave clothes and watch with happy tears as 'Jesus' encountered 'Mary' and we would run back to the house with great joy, shouting, 'He is risen!' and have a wonderful Easter Sunday service followed by a slap-up celebratory lunch. It was all truly moving, entering into the story day by day as it happened.

There was a day between the Friday and the Sunday, though, when nothing happened. Easter Saturday. No acting, no running around the estate excitedly watching dramatic scenes. Just quiet and waiting. Maybe a short talk. Maybe a few crafts.

What I remember most about that day was the feeling of existing in the uncertainty. Even though we knew how the story ended and that everything would be all right on Sunday – Jesus would rise again, as he had the year before and every year before that and as he always did – there was still this almost imperceptible feeling of doubt and wondering what might happen if he didn't. Would Easter

Sunday really arrive? Would it all be OK in the end? What must that first Holy Saturday have been like for those disciples for whom the thought that Jesus would come back to life could not be further from their minds? For them, Good Friday was the end. Failure.

What happened to Jesus on the day between Good Friday and Easter Sunday? Whenever we say the Apostles' Creed, we state that Jesus 'descended into hell', but what did he do there? What took place in that 'failure space' between cross and resurrection?

I like the little saying about Holy Saturday that goes like this. 'What do you think Jesus did on Holy Saturday?' said the priest. 'Well,' said the child, 'I think he went and searched the coldest, darkest corners of hell, looking for his friend Judas.' It's a comforting idea – that Christ descended to hell to bring light and release to the darkest places, such that there is nowhere untouched by the victory of the cross, including our deepest darkest failures.

Although there is little biblical justification for the 'harrowing' of hell, save a few contentious passages,[8] Christian tradition has it that Jesus descended to hell on Holy Saturday to release the captives held there. Among my favourite pieces of art is one of the frescos in the Monastery of San Marco in Florence, which depicts Jesus leading the captives out of hell. So violently has he bashed down the gates that an unfortunate demon who happened to be in the wrong place at the wrong time lies crushed beneath the broken-down door. Irenaeus of Lyon, in the second century, explained that, 'the Lord descended into the regions beneath the earth to preach his advent and to proclaim remission of sins for all who believe in him'.[9] Thomas Aquinas stated that 'it was fitting for Christ to descend into hell . . . as He showed forth His power on earth by living and dying, so also He might manifest it in hell, by visiting it and enlightening it'.[10] So Jesus' mission in hell was to 'harrow' it, to make it holy, to preach to the captives there and to rescue even those who had failed the most. It's a way of looking at Holy Saturday from the point of view of the victory of Easter. Jesus is the victor who strides boldly into hell, setting the captives free, bringing his light and hope. 'Easter is the secured end no matter what. Jesus, in hell, tramples over death. Keys of the kingdom dangle in his hands.'[11]

Another way of looking at the harrowing of hell is to say that Jesus went there so there is no place he had not been to experience the depths of human suffering, even death and hell. It's a view espoused by Catholic theologian Hans Urs von Balthasar who said that Jesus had to enter into every aspect of human experience in order to redeem it, 'only what has been endured by Christ is healed and saved'.[12] That is what the descent into hell was all about, Jesus redeeming the darkest and worst places of suffering. He writes, 'By it Christ takes the existential measure of everything that is sheerly contrary to God, of the entire object of the divine eschatological judgment, which here is grasped in that event in which it is "cast down."'[13] As Shelly Rambo says, 'This non-victorious descent sends a different message: there is no reach of human experience that is unexperienced by God. Not even hell. The cross of

Good Friday narrates this. But the hell of Holy Saturday confirms it.'[14]

The difference between the two approaches lies in whether you tend to see Saturday in the light of Sunday – as the preliminary to victory – or see Saturday in the light of Friday – as the continuation and completion of Christ's suffering.

Whatever conclusion you come to, it's not especially that aspect of Holy Saturday which gives us the most insight into the experience of living with failure. It's the waiting. Again, Jesus prepared his disciples for this aspect of their experience. In John 16.16–17 he tells them, 'A little while, and you will no longer see me, and again a little while, and you will see me.' Those cryptic words, from that side of the cross, understandably baffled his disciples and they asked one another:

'What does he mean by saying to us, "A little while, and you will no longer see me, and again a little while, and you will see me"; and "Because I am going to the Father"?' They said, 'What does he mean by this "a little while"? We do not know what he is talking about.'
(John 16.17–18)

At least they were honest!

The 'little while' could be referring to the time between the Ascension, when Jesus disappeared from their view, and when he will come again in glory, but it could also reference Holy Saturday, when the disciples had to endure

154

the 'little while' of waiting, during which time they would not see him because he was dead, before his resurrection to new life – the 'little while' of Saturday, between Friday and Sunday. David Ford, in his commentary on John's Gospel, writes of this as being:

the most important time in history, the little while during which Jesus is crucified, is dead and seen no longer, is resurrected and seen again, and goes to the Father to begin a new time, that day of utter joy, embracing those sharing his Spirit in an intimacy that can ask anything of the Father in my name.[15]

There's another way of speaking about the 'little while'. When Jesus foretold his own death and resurrection, he often used the description 'three days' to describe the length of time that he would be in the tomb, such as in Matthew 16.21: 'From that time on, Jesus began to show his disciples that he must go to Jerusalem and undergo great suffering at the hands of the elders and chief priests and scribes, and be killed, and on the third day be raised.'[16] His disciples did not comprehend what he was speaking about at this stage, of course, but 'three days' still had great significance for them. Three days was symbolic of waiting for Jewish people; not today or even tomorrow but the day after that – three days. Holy Saturday, the 'little while', the middle day of the three days, as I and my fellow participants in the Passion play at Lee Abbey found, is that experience of 'dead' time – of waiting for something to happen and not knowing whether it is going to or not, and when it does, what it will bring. It is 'the day when our doubt and emptiness and helplessness is honoured in the church calendar; when we sit with our pain and dwell with our uncertainty, unable to fix things or speed them up, but instead clinging on until "the third day" when all will be revealed'.[17] It's the experience of the disciples huddled in the upper room, waiting to find out what on earth they were supposed to do, waiting in the empty space, without the knowledge that there will be a resurrection and what that will mean for them, 'for as yet they did not understand the scripture, that he must rise from the dead' (John 20.9).

It is the disciples' sense of incomprehension that speaks most clearly into our experience of failure – or the fear of it at least. It's the place where we don't know what is going to happen, but we fear the worst. It's the 'we had hoped that he was the one to redeem Israel' of the disciples on the road to Emmaus (Luke 24.21). It's the experience of the young person waiting for exam results or someone waiting for medical test results to come through. It was the experience of many of us during the pandemic, knowing something awful was happening, but not really what it was or how or when it would end, despite the assurances of government and scientists. It is the pause that we do not yet know is a pause rather than the end. There is sadness in that place, uncertainty, the reality of possible failure, yet in that place God remains.

Welsh poet R. S. Thomas has been called a poet of Holy Saturday. His poems speak of the 'purifying silence' of that day, on which 'all speech about God and his engagement with humanity is brought to nothing; or, to use more boldly participatory language, it lies dead in the grave with the Son of God'.[18] Many of Thomas's poems use images of silence, doubt, uncertainty, as opposed to knowledge, faith, confidence. His poem 'Kneeling' expresses Thomas's frustration with words, with ready certainties. It speaks of the importance of the pause:

Prompt me, God;
But not yet. When I speak,
Though it be you who speak
Through me, something is lost.
The meaning is in the waiting.[19]

We are very good at using words to justify our successes and our very existence. Holy Saturday silences all that and is, therefore, the day for this current age. We are living in Holy Saturday times. We do not know what the future holds, not only in relation to the COVID pandemic but also the aftermath of it on our systems and bodies; the war in Ukraine and its effects on the costs of things, most notably fuel and energy, but also grain and oil; the impacts of the environmental crisis playing out not only in the places we always associate with climate catastrophe but also the world over – in the form of drought, floods, rising sea levels.

In the Church, we entered the pandemic with a kind of crisis mentality. There were attempts to predict what the Church would need to be and do to survive and even thrive. There was much talk of what would happen 'after the pandemic', but some three years later, at the time of writing, we're not sure what that will look like still. Predicting anything with certainty at present is extremely difficult and yet we use loads and loads of words to try to do so. It may be that the silence of Holy Saturday, in which the disciples didn't yet know what 'after the crucifixion' would look like, is exactly our experience too. Theologian Alan E. Lewis writes:

If Easter Saturday[20] connotes rupture and termination, a sense of darkness and disintegration, the loss of meaning, hope and creativity, then our culture surely to a significant degree is an Easter Saturday society, in the throes, wittingly or not, of its own demise.[21]

What *does* Holy Saturday say to us about our experience of failure? What does it mean for us to say week by week in our churches 'he descended into hell'? A theology of Holy Saturday is a theology for all who suffer or fail or doubt or cannot see the way ahead.

Pete Greig describes Holy Saturday as 'the no-man's land between the questions and answers, prayers uttered and miracles to come. It's where we wait, with a particular mixture of faith and despair – whenever God is silent or life doesn't make sense.'[22] It's a particular theology for the times we have been through and still live in now. Shelly Rambo describes the experience of medical staff during the pandemic in such terms:

The expanses of hell are our near and present realities. Witnesses gather on one end of the phone calling out to their loved ones in the wilderness of the ICU. There is no compass for this wilderness. If Easter faith is worth anything, it claims that love survives.[23]

This seems to me to be the place where we need to look for a theology of failure. Failure is not something that we 'get over', a temporary inconvenience on the road to great success. It is not something that we can sidestep or dodge, no matter how victorious the resurrection ultimately is.

Failure is something that we need to learn to live with, to dwell in, like Holy Saturday. We need this in-between day. It is the most honest expression of our current human experience. We live constantly in the in-between, in the place where failure of all kinds is a present reality. We live in the now-and-not-yet of the coming kingdom, where great success is promised, of course, eventually, but is definitely not here yet.

For now, we live in failure and that's OK. There is a plan – God has it, not us, and it exists even though often it seems as though things are not going according to any sort of plan at all. All the same, God is with us in that place, on Saturday. The trick is not to try to avoid or skip over Saturday and not to expect Sunday too soon, try to sort things out or say 'failure is really just the road to success' too quickly.

We need also to remember, of course, that Holy Saturday is day two of three. There is something before it and something after it. Holy Saturday exists only because of what Jesus did to end all suffering and failure on Good Friday, while Easter Sunday confirms that the victory has been won. Even as we exist in Saturday, we can do so without fear, because of Friday and Sunday. We say 'he descended into hell', but we also say he 'was crucified, died, and was buried' and then 'on the third day he rose again'. We are people of all three creedal statements, all three days, who live in the little while and, because of all three days, we are held by God, who knows what it is to suffer, who descended to the depths of our human experience and who rose again to bring life. 'In short, to say these words is to declare that we are free – free to love our enemies, to face sin in its stark reality, and to embrace the world without fear of the cost'.[24]

Sometimes we need to stay in Holy Saturday, not because we particularly want to but because there is no other option open to us. Holy Saturday shows us that, even while we are living in the grief and pain of the crucifixion, when Jesus is dead and buried, God is still at work, redeeming our failures. He does this even when we can't see what he is doing or how it will end. Much of life seems to be lived in the gaps between pain and hope, and dwelling in Holy Saturday is the most honest place we could be.

A Holy Saturday Church

What might it mean for the Church to live in Holy Saturday and to embrace failure? Here are a few ways in which living in Holy Saturday may help us as the Church to make sense of these times, which defy sense-making.

First, we are to acknowledge our own limitations. We cannot rely on our own ingenuity, cleverness or strength, because, at present, we have very little of any of these things. R. S. Thomas in 'Kneeling' describes himself, the priest, kneeling before the altar before preaching his sermon:

> the sun's light
> Ringing me, as though I acted
> A great rôle.[25]

Sometimes all we can do is kneel and wait, and not much else, whatever our role: 'Failure is often God's deliverance from the illusion of self-sufficiency, believing more in ourselves than in God.'[26]

Second, Holy Saturday is a day of provisionality: 'We stand within the troubling shadow of the cross, and the final Sunday of history is not yet upon us: it is, of necessity, a day of incompleteness.'[27] This saves us from making our plans too firm, too solid. We need flexibility in our planning.

Third, we make space for failure. When it happens, we don't linger in Good Friday, asking whose fault it is or rush ahead to the victory of Easter Sunday, quickly trying to cover it up and forget it ever happened. Rather, we sit with the disciples on Holy Saturday in the place of wondering and trying to make sense of it.

On the road to Emmaus – which describes the experience of the disciples in the in-between, wondering what had just happened and how it would all turn out – Jesus patiently, slowly, carefully walked with them as they tried to do a post-mortem on the events of recent days and helped them to discover the truth so that they could move on (or, in their case, go back to Jerusalem). He let them pour out their honest feelings to him before gently leading them to understand a bit more. They didn't know it was him, they didn't recognize him, but he was there. They didn't know what was coming up in the future. They definitely hadn't got it all sorted in their heads, but Jesus himself was there with them, walking, explaining, listening, staying. It was only over dinner that night, later, as he broke bread, that their eyes were opened: 'Were not our hearts burning within us . . . ?' (Luke 24.32).

In the end, the answer is always Jesus.

A prayer for Holy Saturday

Hear our prayer for a world still living an Easter Saturday existence, oppressed and lonely, guilty of godlessness and convinced of godforsakenness. Be still tomorrow the God you are today, and yesterday already were: God with us in the grave, but pulling thus the sting of death and promising in your final kingdom an even greater victory of abundant grace and life over the magnitude of sin and death. And for your blessed burial, into which we were baptized, may you be glorified for evermore. Amen.
Alan E. Lewis[28]

For discussion

1 Which of the Gospel passages displaying Jesus' teaching about and attitude to failure speaks to you most and why?

2 In what ways do you see the cross as a failure, and in what ways do you view it as the end of all failures?

3 How does the idea that we are living in 'Holy Saturday' times speak to you? How is this related to Jesus' directive to take up your cross and follow him?

6

How to fail really well

Here is your life. You might never have been, but you are, because the party wouldn't have been complete without you. Here is the world. Beautiful and terrible things will happen. Don't be afraid. I am with you.
Fredrick Buechner, *Beyond Words* (2004)

In this book we have looked failure full in the face, acknowledging that the tendency to fail is an inevitable part of being human. We have considered the many and varied ways in which we can fail, noted how God sees our failures and what he came to do about it, assessed what it means to be part of the failing Church and reflected on Jesus – the greatest 'failure' of them all. Now we need to work out what to do with all that stuff and how to live well with failure in the here and now. I am by no means an expert (OK, I am), but here are some things that may help a person, like you or me, who wishes to see failure not as the end but as the beginning of living life in all its fullness.

Live with the mess

I wonder if we learn more about ourselves from the way we deal with failure than we do almost anything else in life? For instance, I am not very good at living with mess.

Tidying things is my default activity. Especially when I know that I have a difficult task ahead of me (a book to write, for instance), I will engage with obsessive organization as a displacement activity. My house has never been tidier than it has as I've been writing this book. I even tidied my whole linen cupboard the other day, folding each sheet and duvet cover and stacking them carefully according to size and type. It's so beautiful. The trouble is, I tend to try to do with my life what I have just done with my bedlinen – that is, get it all neat and in order – and it's not always possible.

When starting a new role or going into a new situation, I know that I am inclined to try to organize the heck out of it. That's not a bad thing in itself. Sometimes the things I'm involved with (oh, like the Church of England) could do with a little order here and there. But the trouble is, when things then start to become untidy again, as the bedlinen will when I pull duvet covers and sheets out to use them, and as situations do when real people become involved, and as churches and organizations do when people do what people do and mess up and fall out with one another and refuse to behave in the impeccable way in which I would wish them to, I get frustrated and fed up. That's not the way. I need to do what I can to help to improve things, but also learn to live with the mess, because messy failure is an inevitable consequence of living.

Part of the problem with understanding failure is that we are not trained well for it. Parents, rightly, see it as their duty to protect children from harm, and it is never acceptable for a parent or carer to place a child in harm's way, but sometimes we may be inclined to overprotect them, trying to stop anything from going wrong at all.

When failure does, inevitably, come into our children's lives, it's how we react to it that matters. I know with my own children that my tendency is to want to whisk away the problem, to downplay difficulties, to say 'Everything will be OK' – in the hope that speaking those words might make it come true – and to do all in my power to correct what has gone wrong. But children need to learn to see failure as part of the texture of life. The main thing is that they must know they are loved and accepted, whatever failure comes their way. This is all the more important given the pressures placed on them not only to succeed themselves but also to see their success relative to that of others.

Every year in the UK when the A-level and GCSE results come out, there is an accompanying commentary in public discourse about whether this year's results are higher or lower than they were the year before, and what that is supposed to signify. Whole year groups are labelled 'good' or 'bad' depending on their position relative to those of previous years. My husband and I have always made it our practice to 'reward' our children for exam effort rather than exam success, making sure that any gifts or treats are given the day *before* the results come out.

Social media, while being an important means of communication and connection for young people, can also be a source of great anxiety when it looks as though everyone else is having a much better time, with more friends, social opportunities and successes than they are. It is challenging for them to have a healthy sense of what their inside world is like when they are constantly comparing it to everyone else's outside world, and then only the selected bits of that world their friends wish them to see.

We serve our children and young people well if we 'teach them that failure belongs to everyone and that it is possible to be at once kind, clever, idiotic and controlled'.[1] Perhaps we ought to consider introducing 'failure classes' into every parenting course, Christian basics course and Sunday school lesson plan. We would have to use different terminology, of course (ahem), but there is an organization that exists to bring people together to share their failures (F**kUp Nights). Some businesses have started holding regular failure parties to enable employees to share what they have got wrong and how they have learnt from it. A Christian version of these could serve the Church, and especially its young people, very well.

Does the fact that failure has always existed and always will mean that we should resign ourselves to failure and not try to do better? There are two possible reactions to failure and it's possible to go to either of the extremes. One is to pretend that it doesn't exist and to get really upset when anything is less than perfect. The other is to think that all of life is absolutely awful and there's nothing we can do about it.

John Portmann, writing about the existence of sin, says:

Meditation on our repeated failures at virtuous living can lead us to adopt a passive, withdrawn attitude. We give up and resign ourselves to defeat. We adapt to low expectations in a sorry way, blaming our sinfulness on an inability to do any better than failure. Even when conditions become more favourable, we may cling to the safe vision of ourselves as humans who can always be counted on to err.[2]

Young people in particular need to be helped to live with the ups and downs of life and not to assume that, as soon as something goes slightly wrong, all is hopeless. 'Just because this part of life is a struggle, doesn't mean your whole life is a failure' is the message that we need to give them and model in our own lives.

We must be wary, too, of going to other extreme and simply saying, 'Stiff upper lip' and 'Pull yourself together.'

The trick is helping people to deal with life's knock-backs and to become friends with failure. Being able to do this is the definition of resilience – not toughing it out when things are hard but feeling the pain of loss, disappointment and failure *and* being able to accept that reality with the help and love of others. We need to be able to flex with the vagaries of the human experience.

My son is doing an acting course at university. He tells the story of a day when things had gone badly for one of his classmates in a rehearsal. He messed up a scene, it went wrong and he started to cry. As the tears welled up, embarrassed by what was happening, he went to walk out of the rehearsal room, but the teacher gently blocked him from doing so and encouraged him to stay. 'Don't leave,' he said, 'Stay and cry in *this* space, with *these* people. In the space where it went wrong, acknowledge and own the feeling.' The student was brave enough to do as the teacher requested and, as he sat and cried in front of everyone, *with* everyone, he began to experience the release of his anguish at how things had gone, as well as the compassion and support of his fellow actors. 'We all learnt something important that day,' my son said. We need to learn to live well in the mess of this world, to feel failure and the emotions surrounding it, to normalize it, make friends with it and help those around us to do likewise.

So what can we learn about ourselves by living in the mess? One of the things we note is that God is closer to the mess than we may imagine, and our messy lives and world are never beyond the scope of God's love and redemption. Indeed, 'mess' may even be part of God's plan. After all, when God created the earth, he formed it out of chaos.

The words of Genesis 1.2 show clearly that the earth was complete chaos, 'a formless void and darkness covered the face of the deep, while a wind from God swept over the face of the waters'. In Hebrew, the words for 'chaos', 'darkness', 'deep' and 'waters' all held rich resonances of fearful, primordial mess. But note that all this was happening *before* Adam and Eve ate the forbidden fruit and sin entered God's perfect creation. Therefore, although God created order out of chaos, chaos is not bad in and of itself. It needs to be shaped by God, but it is not inherently bad.

Chaos theory, defined as 'the qualitative study of unstable aperiodic behaviour in deterministic nonlinear systems'[3] or, put in simpler terms, 'why when you put a piece of string or your phone headphones in a drawer, they inevitably come out tangled', maintains that unpredictability is built into the universe and we need to learn to live with it. Perhaps, then, we can't insist on too much neatness in life, and chaos is not necessarily beyond the scope of God's plans.

Human failure also teaches us that nothing is beyond the providential care of God. Someone once described life to me as a bit like looking at the back of a tapestry, where all the different loops and ends of wool simply look like a tangled mess. It's only when you turn the tapestry over that you realize that what looked so random from the back is actually a beautiful picture. In God's providence, he sees the beautiful side of the tapestry, and perhaps one day we will, too, but for now we trust that the chaotic tangles of colour that are your life and mine have some meaning beyond that which we can decipher for ourselves this side of heaven.

Abraham Kuyper, the Dutch theologian and one-time prime minister, famously said, 'There is not a square inch in the whole domain of our human existence over which Christ, who is Sovereign over all, does not cry "Mine!"'[4] Kuyper's view was that, although every sphere of life is under the lordship of Christ, we now see only dimly the reality of this truth. That means he is Lord of our failures and we may not see the part they play in the end design this side of eternity. I am not saying that God deliberately makes life difficult ('I know, I'll add a splash of suffering here, a little bit of failure there'). I am simply saying that what to you and me may look like a mess, could, in God's providence, be something beautiful.

Make friends with ordinary

Although failure is a key part of life, and some failures are dramatic, most of life is quite boring. How do we live well when life is not even that messy, simply, well, ordinary?

Our media channels feed us a constant diet of extraordinary and we frequently feel that we are falling short in comparison. One of the reactions against some mission initiatives in the Church of England that found its expression in the Save the Parish[5] movement was a plea in favour of the ordinary. Parishes, for several years, had heard exciting stories of extraordinary growth in churches in places where specific central funding had been given and began to wonder, 'What about my ordinary parish? How will we be sustained and enabled to grow?'

It is good to hear stories of success and to rejoice when things go well. It can be inspiring to hear of growth in churches, people turning to Christ and lives transformed. We need to tell such stories with care, however, as they can act in two very different ways. They can either serve as an inspiration to try something new or lead to people becoming demoralized when they try the same things, perhaps with fewer resources or a different set of circumstances, and don't see the same results. It is good to be inspired by the extraordinary, but we need to be aware that if we set the bar so high, we are bound to see what we have (not) 'achieved' as failure.

Who do we hold up as our heroes? Let me tell you about someone. She was called Gladys Hopkins. Heard of her? No, you won't have. Gladys Hopkins (née Price) was born in the Welsh valleys in 1895. She lived all her life in the small town of Tonmawr, near Neath. When she died in 1998, aged 103, her funeral was held in the same church in which she had been christened, officiated at by her thirteenth vicar. She sat in the same pew her entire life. She worked in service at a country house for a while until she married and had eight children, one of whom, Henry, died in the local coal mine. She lived at home with another of her sons, Tom, until the day she died. Gladys enjoyed a sherry trifle, and preferred salmon 'out of a tin' to fresh. She and Tom grew tomatoes and liked to watch the snooker on TV. She loved to be visited by her children, grandchildren, great-grandchildren and, once, her great, great-granddaughter, into whose palms she would press a five-pound note as they left. She met Prince Charles (as he was then) once, when he came to open a community centre in the village, and there was a framed photo in her living room to prove it. Gladys never travelled far, nor did anything of particular note, yet she lived a good, faithful, Christian life. She was a wife, mother, Christian, church-goer and member of her community, and her impact on the lives of her family and those who knew and loved her – their children and their children's children – cannot be overestimated. Gladys Hopkins was very, very ordinary. She was my great-grandmother. She was a real heroine.

When your get up and go has got up and gone

What about when we're not living on the mountains of dramatic failures or on the level plains of ordinariness, but in the troughs and valleys of apathy?

There is a proverb that says, 'Hope deferred makes the heart sick' (Proverbs 13.12). One of the features of the COVID pandemic was the constant deferral of hope. Dates by which lockdowns were supposed to be lifted came and went. Again and again. Daily, we anxiously saw the numbers rise on the news bulletins – so many cases, so many hospitalizations, so many deaths. We lived day by day, hoping for the end but not really knowing what that might look like when it came. We still don't fully.

We lived for months in a state of heightened awareness of Everything That Was Happening, so is it any wonder that now, after all this time, we are very, very tired and suffering a kind of heartsickness? We used to speak with longing about the 'new normal', but if that ever has transpired, I am not sure what it looks like.

There's a name for this condition: 'acedia' (literally 'lack of care or compassion'), described as a 'strange combination of listlessness, undirected anxiety, and inability to concentrate'.[6] It emerged in the seven deadly sins as 'sloth', but it doesn't exactly equate to laziness. Acedia was a term coined by early monks to describe that combination of listlessness, anxiety and despair they called the 'noonday demon'. Thomas Aquinas identified an 'oppressive sorrow, which, to wit, so weighs upon man's mind, that he wants to do nothing'.[7] Desert Father John Cassian describes the behaviour of a monk suffering acedia:

He looks about anxiously this way and that, and sighs that none of the brethren come to see him, and often goes in and out of his cell, and frequently gazes up at

the sun, as if it was too slow in setting, and so a kind
of unreasonable confusion of mind takes possession
of him like some foul darkness.[8]

If that monk were living today, he would probably be
constantly, mindlessly scrolling through social media. One
of the effects of 'long COVID' is what has been termed
'brain fog', which sounds very like the 'unreasonable
confusion of mind' described by Cassian.

More than the physical, it is the mental and spiritual
effects of acedia that loom largest. Kathleen Norris, in her
book on the subject *Acedia and Me*, describes the feeling
like this: 'When life becomes too difficult and challenging
and engagement with others too demanding, acedia offers
a kind of spiritual morphine: you know the pain is there,
yet you can't rouse yourself to give a damn.'[9]

'Failure' can seem like a very active word. 'Failing' even
more so. What about when your failure is simply not caring
at all? The Bible is no stranger to experiences of acedia, that
feeling of simply wanting to give up. After Nineveh was
spared, Jonah became angry at the mercy of God, 'angry
enough to die' (Jonah 4.9), and sat down under a bush to
have what might be termed an 'almighty strop'. Perhaps it
was an experience of acedia, which includes the inability
to see and receive the goodness of God. Luke describes
how Jesus and disciples went to the Mount of Olives the
night before his death. Jesus prayed with anguish, but
'When he got up from prayer, he came to the disciples and
found them sleeping because of grief' (Luke 22.45). Acedia
may be close to what the disciples were experiencing in

Gethsemane – exhaustion and listlessness born of grief and stress. Perhaps it was acedia that afflicted the church in Laodicea, which is described as being 'neither cold nor hot' (Revelation 3.15). The remedy for this affliction is to welcome Jesus into the mess, the disappointment, the chaos, the ordinary, as he says, 'Listen! I am standing at the door, knocking; if you hear my voice and open the door, I will come in to you and eat with you, and you with me' (Revelation 3.20).

And you don't have to tidy up first.

In every season

I mentioned earlier in this chapter the need for young people to come to terms with failure. It's something that we need to relearn as we get older. There is a particular poignancy to failure as part of the ageing process. It is partly because the older we get, the more likely we are to have failed at many things (as well as succeeded at others), coupled with feelings of regret for choices not made and opportunities missed.

Generally speaking, I am not a person who regrets much – it's not really in my nature and I have much to be thankful for. But I do regret selling a house I owned in 1997 so that I could train at theological college. I regret not speaking to my father for many years. I regret sometimes putting work before my family. I regret the mistakes, large and small, known and unknown, that I have made in the course of my ministry and the pain and hurt and disappointment and confusion they have caused others.

There are also regrets that come with ageing – in itself a failure of sorts. There was a time when I was younger when I genuinely felt that I could do anything, given the time and resources. There was, even into my thirties and forties, still a remote possibility that I could train to be a surgeon or run a marathon or learn how to water-ski, but now I'm in my fifties, those possibilities are steadily fading as the years continue to go by. Our bodies begin to fail – energy levels are lower than they were, bones creak and ache, everything migrates south. Someone once said that you know you are ageing when you begin to make the same sounds getting out of a chair that you once made during sex!

For many years I took my health and energy for granted. When, last year, an extreme reaction to the COVID vaccine landed me in hospital for a week, with consequent effects that lasted for several months, I began to feel older. Suddenly, things seem not to be working as well as they did. Joe Moran says reassuringly, 'No shame should attach to this kind of failure, for it comes to us all. Everyone alive is exposed and susceptible – walking wounded. You may chase success in the belief that you are immortal; but, by virtue of being alive, you have already failed.'[10] I do find that strangely comforting.

I reckon there is a time, usually around 45 to 50 years old, when you suddenly realize that there are no grown-ups any more, because now, apparently, you are the grown-up. Because I went into ordained ministry relatively young, for years I was the youngest at absolutely every church event I went to. Now that's not the case and there are younger, brighter people all around. I am supposed to be the adult now, but I feel very ill-equipped for that role, if I'm honest. I keep on looking for the person who's supposed to be in charge in the room before realizing that it's probably me.

Owning up to this state of affairs is the first step towards winning the battle with regret. Psychologists Laura King and Joshua Hicks explain the maturity that comes with being grown up: 'maturity depends on the adult's capacity to confront lost goals, or lost possible selves, and acknowledge regrets and sorrows over roads not taken or dreams unfulfilled.'[11] Being an adult means taking responsibility for the failures and regrets of the past, but not allowing them to swamp us or define our present or our future.

Fail widely (learn to make different kinds of mistakes)

I have learnt some things from my failures and mistakes. It's best to check very carefully the date of your holiday booking so that you don't arrive at the ferry port 24 hours early with nowhere to stay overnight and tired children in the back of the car. If you drive too close to dry stone walls in Cumbria at night, you get a double puncture, possibly in a remote place where there's no mobile phone signal. If you don't check documents you receive by email carefully enough, even at very busy times, you overlook things that will later cause harm and confusion. Does that mean I won't make mistakes again? No, it simply means that I won't make *those* mistakes again.

One of the things most often said is that failure presents an opportunity to learn and to do things differently.

Indeed, as we saw in Chapter 1, most aphorisms about failure identify this as its major benefit. If you do an Internet search for 'quotes about failure' – even better, click on the 'images' filter – you'll be treated to screen after screen of mountains and seascapes overlain with quotes saying exactly that, in different ways (mostly attributed to people who have been wildly successful in their lives): 'Success consists of going from failure to failure without loss of enthusiasm' (wrongly attributed to Winston Churchill); 'If you're not prepared to be wrong, you'll never come up with anything original'; 'It's fine to celebrate success but it is more important to heed the lessons of failure'; 'Do not be embarrassed by your failures, learn from them and start again.' We're supposed to learn from our failures and become better people as a result, not do them again.

But it's not that easy, is it?

The premise of this book is that failure is an inevitable part of human life and so we need to acknowledge and live well with it. Sometimes we learn from mistakes. Sometimes we fail at that, too, and do not. The Bible is full of people who seemed never to learn from their mistakes, making the same ones again and again, driven by their own 'besetting sins' (more of that below). You would think that Jacob, for example, would have learnt from his own childhood experience of rejection not to have favourites, but he managed to alienate most of his children by his preferential treatment of Joseph, then, later on, Benjamin. David makes his sin with Bathsheba worse by trying to cover it up and kill her husband Uriah. Peter appears not to have learnt the lessons of hasty and ill-advised speaking, denying knowing Jesus three times. Like these biblical heroes of the faith, sometimes we learn our failure lessons and sometimes we don't.

One of the things that I am aware of as a parent is that I try not to make the same mistakes that my parents (being human) made with me. I have, however, made plenty of new and unique ones with my own children. Someone once said, 'Insanity is doing the same thing over and over again and expecting different results.' (Incidentally, this quotation is often attributed to Albert Einstein, but he never said it, so perhaps insanity is attributing a quotation to the wrong person over and over again.) In the case of failure, we may not make the same errors over and over again, but our repertoire is endless.

Learning from failure is different from turning failure into success. You may simply learn not to mess things up so badly, or in the same way, next time. You may learn how to make life, if not incredibly successful, perhaps a little more tolerable. Perhaps we need to set the bar quite low when it comes to learning from failure. As Moran says, '"Fail better" doesn't mean, keep trying, or even, "fail a little less catastrophically next time". It means you must bear to go on, hauling your body into each new day, when you know that you will fail and fail again.'[12]

We know that failure is wrong. It often hurts other people and us, so we have a deep instinct not to fail and will want to put things right when we do. Consider the number of foundations and charities set up in the wake of great failure and tragedy by the relatives of those affected, 'in order to stop anyone else having to go through what we did'. Yet, because we are human and sinfulness in all its forms, sometimes personal, sometimes corporate, has affected the whole of the human condition, we know that we cannot eradicate failure completely, no matter what lengths we go to mitigate its effects. So perhaps we need simply to try not to make the *same* mistakes all the time. Enlarge your repertoire of failure and become aware of what mistakes you are most likely to make, because you're you, and try to make different ones next time.

To do that, you may need to . . .

Know your besetting sins

The way to be a person who fails really well is to be self-aware of the ways in which you are most likely to fail, and the things that are most likely to cause you to do so, then work with others towards owning both and speaking about it with kindness to yourself when it happens.

I studied English at university and there fell in love with Shakespeare. When I try to assess what it is about Shakespeare's plays and sonnets that draws me in, it is the language, of course, and the comedy and the turn of phrase, but most of all it is the observation of human nature. We can see ourselves in Shakespeare's characters at different stages of our lives.

My favourite play is *King Lear*, which may seem an odd choice, until I tell you that it helped me to make sense of my own family life at a difficult time. I had a strained relationship with my father, who demanded outward expressions of my love in the same way that Lear does of his daughters and, eventually, he had a series of breakdowns, as Lear does. I read Cordelia's speech to her father at my dad's funeral: 'Good my lord, You have begot me, bred me, lov'd me; I return those duties back as are right fit, Obey you, love you, and most honour you.'[13]

We can see in Shakespeare's protagonists flaws of character that lead, inevitably, inexorably, towards the oft fatal consequences of the drama. In Greek tragedy, coined first in Aristotle's *Poetics*,[14] these character flaws or defects are termed *hamartia* – the same word used most often in the New Testament for sin, as we saw in Chapter 3. Macbeth and Lady Macbeth are driven by the *hamartia* of ambition, Othello is riven with jealousy, King Lear suffers from pride and insecurity, Julius Caesar from the love of power. These 'archetypes' are so universal that some leadership training organizations use Shakespeare's characters and their speeches and interactions as the basis for explorations into the culture of teams and other leadership skills.[15]

Mercifully, not many of us have the kinds of character traits that lead us to murder royalty, reject our children or bump off any who try to stand in the way of our quest for power, but my guess is that many of us are aware of aspects of our personality and make-up that get us into trouble and cause us to fail in manifold ways, again and again. Hebrews 12.1 speaks of 'the sin that clings so closely', translated in the King James Version as 'sin which doth so easily beset us'.

'Besetting' sins are those aspects of our own character that lead us to fall in the same way repeatedly. Knowing what those flaws are and being aware of the impact they have on our interactions is half the battle. Where they are unacknowledged, they are at their most powerful. Indeed, a lack of self-awareness is most likely to cause me to fail and make mistakes. This includes our own conscious and unconscious biases, so we need others to help us to do this gently, lovingly and patiently.

Among the benefits of what Gregory Jones and Kevin Armstrong call 'holy friendships' is that such friends 'challenge the sins we have come to love'.[16] Owning up to the fact that it is besetting sins that are liable constantly to cause us to fail can be liberating. Accepting the fact that mistakes were made, and allowing and acknowledging the feelings that raises in us with grief and compassion rather than denial, anger and rage, means we are able to learn from our failings and turn that learning into wisdom.

The way to deal with the 'cognitive dissonance' we explored in Chapter 2 – when we try to avoid owning up to mistakes and failures due to the fear of what they will reveal about us – is to articulate the cognitions and keep them distinct. We need to say, 'When I, a decent, smart person, make a mistake, I remain a decent, smart person, and the mistake remains a mistake. Now, how do I remedy what I did?'[17]

Allow others to fail

The antidote to the shame that is invariably experienced when we fail is to get it out into the open. C. S. Lewis spoke about friendship being born the moment one person says to another, 'What? You too? I thought I was the only one.'[18] The strength of the #MeToo movement was in women speaking out about their experiences of sexual violence and realizing that what had happened to them was, tragically, common to many. There is something very powerful in realizing that you are not alone, and this is no less true when it comes to admitting failure.

Being aware of our own failures means that we are more likely to forgive those of others. Once, I led a training event for a group of senior church leaders on the notion of failure and how to deal well with it. At the end of the session, I invited the participants to break up into small groups if they wished and tell one another about a mistake that they had made and what they thought they had learnt from it. I let them know before the session that this would be on the programme and everyone could choose what they wanted to say to their group. No one had to own up to anything that they didn't feel comfortable sharing. It was quite a risk and I was nervous about how it might go.

I went first and told the gathered room about a mistake that I had made (quite a bad one, actually), then invited them to do the same in smaller groups. I was pleased and humbled to see how these people, all of whom hold senior positions and are constantly in the public glare, carefully and honestly shared with one another times when they had got something wrong. Afterwards, several expressed how cathartic the session had been.

Sharing our failures is not easy and there are not many safe places in which to do so, for all the reasons we've explored, but if there were more we could well be happier people in healthier organizations. One of the benefits of sharing our failures is that it gives permission for others to do the same and be open about it, learning from what has happened.

Imagine what life would look like if we truly allowed others to fail, just as we do. Of course, I am not suggesting here that we actively encourage harmful failure or we do not accept the consequences of our actions when things do go wrong, but imagine if failure was not something shameful that we sought to hide in ourselves and instantly abhorred in others. Imagine if social media was like this. Imagine if job interviews asked you about this, and you didn't have to make up something that sounds really good disguised as something really bad. How much of an encouragement would that be?

A good interview question is, 'Tell us about a time something you did went wrong and what you learnt from it.' A better question would be, 'Tell us about something that is going wrong for you right now and you are still struggling with. What are you doing to help with that?'

How do we allow our public figures to fail? What is the place of accountability, of forgiveness? Hebrews 13.7 encourages God's people to 'remember your leaders, those who spoke the word of God to you; consider the outcome of their way of life, and imitate their faith'. What I like about this is that it doesn't say 'imitate their way of life and consider their faith', it's the other way around. We are to look at what our leaders do, watch them, consider how they live, presumably with all its strengths and weaknesses, ups and downs, failures and successes (because they're human), but only to imitate one thing about them – their faith.

We live in a world that loves to categorize things as 'good' or 'bad' and is very quick to rush to judgement when someone is deemed to have failed. The fact is, though, that we are neither 'good' nor 'bad'. We are all 'good but broken'. So what do we do when we discover the misdemeanors of others? Don't rush to judgement. Stop and wait for the evidence. Carol Tavris and Elliot Aronson advise, 'We can try to balance sympathy and scepticism. And then we can learn to hold our conclusions lightly, lightly enough so that we can let them go if justice demands that we do.'[19]

Earlier in this book we explored the 'works of the flesh' listed in Galatians 5.19–21. In verse 13, Paul encourages the people of God to 'become slaves to one another'. This is difficult language that doesn't sit very comfortably with our abhorrence of slavery of any kind, but what Paul is encouraging here is for us to be accountable for and to one another. In the list of fruits of the Spirit that follows the vices, one fruit given is 'patience' (v. 22). Another translation is 'long-suffering'. The Catholic theologian and Jesuit priest John Navone (whom Pope Francis cites as one of his theological influences), describes this quality:

> Because all human beings are limited, our love must be a patient love. In fact, patience is the first quality of Christian love Paul affirms because it is foundational (1 Cor. 13:4). Patient love is not passive; rather, it is affirming, hopeful and supportive, like that of loving

parents with their toddlers and that of teachers with their students. Patience is the sign of true love because it loves others as the finite, limited persons they truly are.[20]

Patience is putting up with one another's sins, mistakes, weaknesses, failures – sometimes for a very long time. It is about making room for repentance, which may not happen overnight. Patience is the space after failure. One of the prayers of absolution we sometimes pray is that God may give the penitent 'time for amendment of life'.[21] Imagine if we gave one another that time, as well as God giving it to us? Patience is a quality that is not much in evidence in many of our organizations today, including the Church, but it is absolutely crucial to the flourishing of a healthy community of failures.

Know how to lose an argument

One of the skills that we most need to learn to live well with failure is how to be wrong. The realization that you may be wrong about something happens most often after you've had an argument with someone else about it. Arguing well is necessary, and is a lost art. Let's think about why that is.

In this fast-paced digital age, we are used to taking in information quickly as our eyes glance over images as we scroll and they make their way up a phone screen. Our attention span lasts only as long as the speed at which our thumbs can move to take us to one thing and then the next. Information comes in bite-sized pieces and pictures last only as long as we are viewing them. In a world where we type with our clumsy digits on a small screen, messages are necessarily short and we have become easily bored. To communicate, we need to do so quickly, before attention is lost. Whereas adverts of the past would have used many words to extoll the benefits of a product, I saw an advert on TV the other night for a well-known soft drink that consisted entirely of images and accompanying sounds (slurping, mostly), no words at all. We're losing patience with words. Plays, traditionally, are based on words, performed on a stage once a night at 7.30 p.m. with an extra matinée on Saturdays. Words are necessary when no one is close enough to the stage to pick up a twitch of the eyebrow or a pained look. You have to rely on the words to communicate the point, often in long speeches. When your competition is a world of short bites of close-up action or emojis that can be viewed on a personal screen whenever you choose, the world of theatre is discovering that if it wants to attract and keep audiences, especially of younger people, all the senses need to be appealed to.

This is all well and good, but words, unfashionable though they may be, are necessary sometimes, especially if you want to have an argument. You can argue simply with grunts, as many a teenager knows, but it's more fun if you use words. There used to be tradition, which still exists in some more prestigious universities, of debating. The whole aim in debating is to try to win an argument, but it's like a sport. You train, you adopt certain skills and techniques, you use tools of rhetoric and, particularly, employ verbal flourishes to convince a watching audience that your argument is more plausible than your opponent's. This is arguing at its most staged.

An unfortunate consequence of our fast-paced, easily bored, image-based consciousness is that, now, to convince someone you are right or have a cause worth following, you need to grab attention . . . and fast. Titles of movements need sharp, pointed slogans that present the essence of what is being argued without much room for nuance, such as Defund The Police (which is not about withholding funding from the police but, rather, about investing in schemes and interventions that could make crime, and therefore the need for policing, less prevalent), Extinction Rebellion, Black Lives Matter and so on. Behind their headline names, these organizations represent nuanced propositions and ideas, but it's hard to be subtle in one or two words, so their purposes can easily be misunderstood. I wonder if the consequence of this development is that arguments very quickly polarize towards their extremes. 'Quick! Grab my attention, but don't bother taking time to explain the graded nuance of your proposition, still less give time to listening to mine!'

A further consequence is that everyone becomes either solely good or solely bad. There can be no in between. Russia (all of it) is bad and Ukraine (all of it) is good. Amber Heard is bad and Johnny Depp is good (or vice versa). We see this also in the Church. Evangelicals are bad and Liberals are good (or vice versa). But it's rarely as simple as that.

The world seems to be a very angry place at present, which is not surprising when you consider what we're up against. One of the skills that it would be really good for Christians to develop, however, is to get good at seeing the complexities and nuances of an argument and learning to listen well to the perspectives of those with whom you disagree. The highest compliment from someone who disagrees with you is not, 'You are right', it's 'You made me think.'

Stephen Pinker, Johnstone Family Professor of Psychology at Harvard University, argues that the purpose of an argument is not to win, but to enlarge and clarify your understanding of the world: 'We can all promote reason by changing the mores of intellectual discussion, so people treat their beliefs as hypotheses to be tested rather than slogans to be defended.'[22] Good arguments help us to recognize complexity where we once saw simplicity and error. The purpose of proper debate is not consensus, it's the promotion of critical thinking. When someone disagrees with me, does it make me angry or interested? Perhaps we need training in how to be wrong.

Feel the fear and do it anyway

'The fear of failure is every bit as serious and painful as failure itself.'[23] Failure, as we have seen, is a universal experience that we must learn to live with. Fear of failure is not. It's natural to fear the consequences of failing and to do what we can to avoid it, but when that fear becomes the guiding impulse for doing (or not doing) things, then we begin to live lives less full than they might otherwise be.

If you think about it, most of life involves taking risks. We could get mown down by a car that mounts the pavement as we walk along it. If we overwhelmingly feared that unlikely eventuality, we'd never leave the house. The fear of failure can be crippling, so we need constantly to assess appropriate risks and decide which things we are willing to try despite the possibility of failure (walking along the pavement) and which we are not (in my case, skiing).

I often hear talk of leaders in the Church being 'risk averse'. I don't think that descriptor is entirely fair. Different people have different levels of awareness of the possibilities and consequences of failure. In times of uncertainty, such as we are living in now, simply getting out of bed in the morning can seem like a fairly risky proposition. Perhaps this is exactly the right time to try new things and be prepared for failure, because, honestly, what have we got to lose?

In his book *The Innovator's Dilemma*, Clayton Christensen explores why companies fail and why it is difficult for established companies to embrace so-called 'disruptive technologies' that eventually corner the market. Think of companies like Xerox and IBM that, he says, have failed to keep up with innovative technologies and so faded into history as a result. His contention is that when a business is planning for new products, a new approach needs to be taken which embraces and plans for failure: 'Don't bet all your resources on being right the first time. Think of your initial efforts at commercializing a disruptive technology as learning opportunities. Make revisions as you gather data.'[24] I know (and I want to say this very clearly) that the Church is not the same as the business world and 'cornering new markets' does not represent what the Church is about when it tries something new, but perhaps some of the same principles may apply nevertheless. When we do anything new, in business or the Church, as in life generally, a new approach is required and that involves the risk of potential failure.

The Church of England is making plans to invest in lots and lots of new worshipping communities, often initiated by lay people. That in itself is quite a risk. It may go wrong and not go according to plan, but maybe that won't happen and we may consider it a risk worth taking. We need to be prepared for the fact that there will be failures on the way. Some church plants will not 'work' and may not grow into thriving worshipping communities. But some will, and we should recall Jesus' own rate of return in the parable of the sower. One church planter has written about how he came to terms with failure. He says the first step is to acknowledge the inevitability of failure:

> Knowing that I am a failure has also freed me from the fear of taking risks. I am by nature a risk-averse person. Doing an entrepreneurial assessment to see if I had the right temperament to be a church planter, I scored poorly. This hasn't stopped me from being a church planter, though, because it doesn't feel like a risk. Knowing that I will fail means I don't need to fear failure. It is Christ who works in us and through us, so I can trust him and do what he has

put before me. I will fail, but he will succeed in and through me.[25]

A good question to ask in any situation is 'What would I do if I were not afraid?' I wonder if, in the Church, our fear of failure prevents us from trying new things and so we trundle on with what we know and is safe and predictable. John Navone laments that 'fear of failure too often condemns us to mediocrity'.[26] There is a need to analyse what is at the root of our fears. Is it the fear that we risk hurting someone else or ourselves? That is a fear worth listening to. Is it the fear of shame or embarrassment that, if something doesn't go right, we may look stupid? That is a fear we need to analyse further. Lucio in Shakespeare's *Measure for Measure* says, 'Our doubts are traitors and make us lose the good we oft might win by fearing to attempt.'[27]

Play the fool

Despite the mess, life is quite funny, no? There is a close relationship, often overlooked, between the failures, tragedies, mistakes and mess-ups of life and the role of humour. Humour is one of the ways in which we cope when things go wrong. That's why Shakespeare's darkest tragedies invariably include a fool character, whose task it is to offer commentary, often the most truthful words spoken in the plays, when things are going really badly for the main characters. They are also there to provide some light relief for the audience from all the grimness.

So it is the Fool in *King Lear* who speaks the truth about Lear's banishment by his daughters: 'Truth's a dog must to kennel; he must be whipp'd out',[28] while Feste provides a biting commentary on the foibles of the main characters in *Twelfth Night*: 'Better a witty fool than a foolish wit.'[29]

There used to be a day in the church calendar called the Feast of Fools, until it was eventually banned. On that occasion a child would be made bishop and fun would be poked at various ecclesiastical rituals. There is an important role for fools in the Church – those who tell the truth and show up pomposity for what it is, with humour. Terry Eagleton suggests that there is, at the heart of the Christian gospel, a kind of carnivalesque bathos:

> Jesus enters Jerusalem, the stronghold of Roman imperial power on the back of a donkey, and having been deserted by his comrades will be left to face an ignominious death, one reserved by the Romans for political rebels alone. Yet the folly of the cross proves wiser than the wisdom of the philosophers. The intimidatory power of the Law is overthrown, the meek inherit the earth, the sublime became human flesh and blood, the most sacred truths are cast in a plain idiom intended for fishermen and small farmers, and weakness proves the only durable form of strength.[30]

When it comes to dealing well with failure, seeing the funny side is essential. How many tense situations can be diffused with well-timed humour? In their book *Humor, Seriously*, Stanford University researchers Jennifer Aaker and Naomi Bagdonas cite a 2013 Gallup study of 1.4 million people across 166 countries who were asked a simple question: 'Did you smile or laugh a lot yesterday?' Those between the ages of 16 and 23 said 'Yes'. After the age of 23, the answer was 'No'.[31] Aaker's and Bagdonas's contention is that, with age, we unlearn how to laugh at life. They say that organizations would be better if we all learnt to smile a bit more. In a similar vein, John Portmann notes in relation to emotional reactions to adversity that:

> We do 'get over it' as the popular saying goes (at the risk of providing wrongdoers with a ready defense for having harmed us). Humor bubbles up within us, even in bad times, and letting it spin out can be therapeutic. There's nothing humorous about sin, but there's something wondrous about the idea that we can forgive both ourselves and others.[32]

Perhaps we need to recover the role of the fool in life and especially in the Church – that character who makes others laugh even in the face of great failure and, in doing so, is a truth-teller.

Remember that failure is never final

God looks at us differently from the way we see ourselves. We're in very good company, together with others who have failed but whom God is able to use to help him with his purposes. Take a look at the list of 'heroes' of the faith in Hebrews 11 – a list that could have been written very differently.

- By failure Noah got drunk and embarrassed himself in front of his children.
- By failure Abraham sold his own wife to a despotic ruler to save himself.
- By failure Sarah gave her maid to Abraham to bear children rather than trust God's promise.
- By failure Jacob lied to steal his brother's birthright.
- By failure Joseph was proud and boastful.
- By failure Moses killed an Egyptian soldier and fled to the desert.
- By failure Gideon, Barak, Samson and Jephthah, David and Samuel and the prophets were arrogant and indiscreet, failed to trust God and asked constantly for signs, slept with the wrong people and sacrificed their families.

Yet, rather than be known by their failures, they are commended for their faith, which is 'the assurance of things hoped for, the conviction of things not seen' (Hebrews 11.1–2). It is our faith in God's hopeful future in Christ that defines us, not our failures. Indeed, we are not defined by our failures any more than we're defined by our successes.

There is a television programme in the UK that has gained a great deal of popularity in recent years. It's called *The Repair Shop*. The premise of the programme is that people bring to the workshop anything they have that is of sentimental value to them but has been damaged or become shabby and is in need of repair. They explain what the items are and why they matter to them. A panel of expert repairers then set about restoring the items to their former glory, sewing up frayed seams, applying a fresh coat of paint, polishing tarnished metal, fixing mechanisms. At the end of the programme the owners come back to reclaim their objects, which now look as good as new. Tears often ensue, from owners, repairers – and viewers – as everyone marvels at how something so precious and yet broken could be made so shiny and beautiful.

What if we viewed the way God deals with our failures in the same way? We've all messed up. We're broken. We have got things wrong and damaged ourselves and others. But what if God's promise was to take all that and slowly, carefully, painstakingly, with our help and cooperation, put things right again? That may mean giving us the courage to own up to what has gone wrong in the first place; it may mean conversations and counselling to work on that particular *hamartia* and its root cause; it may mean a hard conversation we've been putting off having for a while; it may mean a letter of (genuine, heartfelt) apology; it may simply mean being kinder to ourselves. When things are broken by failure, the answer is not to throw them out with the rubbish but work on repairing them, restoring them.

We are a failing people, but our failures remind us that we long for a day when there will be no more failure, when 'the home of God is among mortals. He will dwell with them; they will be his peoples, and God himself will be with them and be their God; he will wipe every tear from their eyes. Death will be no more; mourning and crying and pain will be no more, for the first things have passed away' (Revelation 21.3–4). Failure is among those 'first things', and our God is in the business of making all things new.

A last word on failure

When you are feeling down about your failures, remember the Benedictine monk who found that, due to cold, damp weather, his carefully stored wine had begun to ferment a second time, creating within it bubbles of carbon dioxide. What a failure! Discovering that mistake must have been a very bad day for him.

The name of the monk?

Dom Perignon.

Cheers, you lovely failures! God bless you.

For discussion

1 What relationship do you see between the mess of your life and God's providence?
2 How do you learn from failure and how is this connected to awareness of your besetting sins?
3 How does the suggestion to accept others' failure but not to define them by their failure appeal to you? What would the consequences of this be in your life?

Notes

1 Why I wrote this book – or 'success and failure revisited'

1 E. Ineson, *Ambition: What Jesus said about power, success and counting stuff* (London: SPCK, 2019).

2 Archbishops' Anti-Racism Taskforce, 'From lament to action: The report of the Archbishops' Anti-Racism Taskforce (London: Church of England), <www .churchofengland.org/sites/default/files/2021-04 /FromLamentToAction-report.pdf> (accessed 20 May 2022).

3 Archbishops' Anti-Racism Taskforce, 'From lament to action', p. 10.

4 News, 'Archbishop of Canterbury apologises to Indigenous peoples of Canada', The Archbishop of Canterbury, The Church of England (2 May 2022), <www .archbishopofcanterbury.org/news/news-and-statements /archbishop-canterbury-apologises-indigenous-peoples -canada> (accessed 12 October 2022).

5 J. Moran, *If You Should Fail: A book of solace* (London: Penguin Random House, 2021), p. 7.

6 L. Himid, 'The art of failure', Tate (3 October 2018), <www .tate.org.uk/art/artists/lubaina-himid-2356/art-failure> (accessed 5 September 2022).

7 A. C. Edmondson, 'Strategies for learning from failure', *Harvard Business Review* magazine (April 2011), <https://

hbr.org/2011/04/strategies-for-learning-from-failure>
(accessed 1 September 2022).

 8 The School of Life, *On Failure: How to succeed at defeat* (London: The School of Life, 2022), p. 84.

 9 J. C. Maxwell, *Failing Forward: Turning mistakes into stepping stones for success* (Nashville, TN: Thomas Nelson, 2000), p. 13.

10 Maxwell, *Failing Forward*, p. 19.

11 The Church of England, 'A commination or denouncing of God's anger and judgements against sinners', Book of Common Prayer, The Church of England (n.d.), <www.churchofengland.org/prayer-and-worship/worship-texts-and-resources/book-common-prayer/commination> (accessed 12 October 2022).

12 The Church of England, 'A commination or denouncing of God's anger and judgements against sinners'.

13 J. McDermott, 'Feel like you've failed this Lent? Maybe that's the point', *America: The Jesuit Review of Faith & Culture* (5 April 2022), <www.americamagazine.org/faith/2022/04/05/lent-resolution-failure-242760> (accessed 5 September 2022).

14 The School of Life, *On Failure*, p. 9.

2 What is failure?

 1 Mischief, at: <www.mischiefcomedy.com> (accessed 12 October 2022).

 2 C. Feltham, *Failure* (London: Routledge, 2012), p. 95.

 3 J. C. Maxwell, *Failing Forward: Turning mistakes into stepping stones for success* (Nashville, TN: Thomas Nelson, 2000), p. 18.

4 J. E. Zull, *From Brain to Mind: Using neuroscience to guide change in education* (Sterling, VA: Stylus, 2011).

5 M. Mills, '"We had such trust, we feel such fools": How shocking hospital mistakes led to our daughter's death', *The Guardian* online (3 September 2022), <www.theguardian.com/lifeandstyle/2022/sep/03/13-year-old-daughter-dead-in-five-weeks-hospital-mistakes?CMP=Share_iOSApp_Other> (accessed 3 September 2022).

6 Health and Safety Executive, 'Leadership and worker involvement toolkit', Health and Safety Executive (n.d.), <www.hse.gov.uk/construction/lwit/index.htm> (accessed 4 September 2022).

7 E. Vanderheiden and C.-H. Mayer (eds), *Mistakes, Errors and Failures across Cultures: Navigating potentials* (Cham, Switzerland: Springer, 2020), p. 3.

8 E. Day, *Failosophy: A handbook for when things go wrong* (London: HarperCollins, 2020), p. 13.

9 Oxford Learner's Dictionaries online, <www.oxfordlearnersdictionaries.com/definition/english/failure> (accessed 3 September 2022).

10 Cambridge Dictionary online, <https://dictionary.cambridge.org/dictionary/english/failure> (accessed 3 September 2022).

11 Feltham, *Failure*, p. 17.

12 R. Parker, *Free to Fail* (London: Triangle, 1998), p. vi.

13 J. Moran, *If You Should Fail: A book of solace* (London: Penguin Random House, 2021), p. 155.

14 A. C. Edmondson, *The Fearless Organization: Creating psychological safety in the workplace for learning, innovation, and growth* (Hoboken, NJ: John Wiley, 2019), p. 163.

15 A. C. Edmondson, 'Strategies for learning from failure', *Harvard Business Review* magazine (April 2011), <https://hbr.org/2011/04/strategies-for-learning-from-failure> (accessed 1 September 2022).

16 Edmondson, 'Strategies for learning from failure'.

17 Edmondson, 'Strategies for learning from failure'.

18 Edmondson, 'Strategies for learning from failure'.

19 B. Brown, *The Gifts of Imperfection* (London: Vermilion, 2020), p. 53.

20 Moran, *If You Should Fail*, p. 14.

21 B. Brown, quoted in J. R. Briggs, *Fail: Finding hope and grace in the midst of ministry failure* (Downers Grove, IL: InterVarsity Press, 2014), p. 77.

22 C. Tavris and E. Aronson, *Mistakes Were Made (but Not by Me): Why we justify foolish beliefs, bad decisions and hurtful acts* (London: Pinter & Martin, 2020), p. 17.

23 Edmondson, 'Strategies for learning from failure'.

24 Tavris and Aronson, *Mistakes Were Made (but Not by Me)*, p. 296.

25 Headteacher, quoted in M. Syed, *Black Box Thinking: Marginal gains and the secrets of high performance* (London: John Murray, 2016), p. 285.

26 Syed, *Black Box Thinking*, p. 294.

27 The School of Life, *On Failure: How to succeed at defeat* (London: The School of Life, 2022), p. 70.

28 S. Beckett, *Company / Ill Seen Ill Said / Worstward Ho / Stirrings Still* (London: Faber and Faber, 2009), p. 11.

29 M. Sayer, *A Non-anxious Presence: How a changing and complex world will create a remnant of renewed Christian leaders* (Chicago, IL: Moody 2022), p. 157.

30 D. Bonhoeffer, *The Cost of Discipleship* (London: SCM Press, 2015), p. 89.

31 J. J. Navone, *Triumph through Failure: A theology of the cross* (Eugene, OR: Wipf & Stock, 1984), p. 23.

32 Navone, *Triumph through Failure*, p. 43.

33 Brother Tristram, *Exciting Holiness: Collects and readings for the festivals and lesser festivals of the calendar of the Church of England* (Norwich: Canterbury Press, 2007).

34 A. Gorman, *The Hill We Climb: An inaugural poem for the country* (London: Chatto & Windus, 2021).

3 Sin, guilt and human nature: towards an imperfect theology of failure (sort of)

1 J. Calvin (H. Beveridge, trans.), *Institutes of the Christian Religion* (Peabody, MA: Hendrickson, 2009), 2.1.8.

2 C. Feltham, *Failure* (London: Routledge, 2012), p. 75.

3 J. Portmann, *A History of Sin: Its evolution to today and beyond: How evil changes, but never goes away* (Lanham, MD: Rowman & Littlefield, 2007), p. 4.

4 A. Solzhenitsyn (T. P. Whitney and H. Willetts, trans.), *The Gulag Archipelago 1918–56: An experiment in literary investigation* (abridged) (London: Vintage, 2018), p. 615.

5 Liturgy Office, England and Wales, 'Rite of penance: Introduction', excerpts from the Rite of Penance 1974, 1975, International Commission on English in the Liturgy Inc. (London: Liturgy Office, England and Wales, 1975), <www.liturgyoffice.org.uk/Resources/Penance/Penance-Intro.pdf> (accessed 14 August 2022).

6 C. C. Black, 'Synoptic Gospels', in K. L. Johnson and D.

Lauber (eds), *T&T Clark Companion to the Doctrine of Sin* (London: Bloomsbury T&T Clark, 2018), pp. 61–78 and 65.

7 D. Konstan, *The Origin of Sin: Greece and Rome, early Judaism and Christianity* (London: Bloomsbury Academic, 2022), p. 102.

8 I. A. McFarland, 'Original sin', in K. L. Johnson and D. Lauber (eds), *T&T Clark Companion to the Doctrine of Sin*, (London: Bloomsbury T&T Clark, 2018), p. 303.

9 McFarland, 'Original sin', p. 306.

10 St Basil the Great, *Detailed Rule for Monks* (resp. 2.1: PG 31.908–910), quoted in Portmann, *A History of Sin*, p. 188.

11 Augustine (H. Bettenson, trans.), *City of God* (London: Penguin, 1972), pp. 14 and 28.

12 P. Fredriksen, *Sin: The early history of an idea* (Princeton, NJ: Princeton University Press, 2012), p. 117.

13 Augustine, *City of God*, 21.12.

14 Community of the Cross of Nails, 'Growing together in hope' (n.d.), <www.coventrycathedral.org.uk/uploads /media/Coventry-Cross-of-Nails-Oct-19-HI-RES.pdf> (accessed 12 October 2022).

15 Community of the Cross of Nails, 'Growing together in hope'.

16 Portmann, *A History of Sin*, xix.

17 Portmann, *A History of Sin*, xvi.

18 J. J. Navone, *Triumph through Failure: A theology of the cross* (Eugene, OR: Wipf & Stock, 1984), p. 96.

19 J. M. Bergen, *Ecclesial Repentance: The churches confront their sinful pasts* (London: T&T Clark, 2011), p. 79.

20 Bergen, *Ecclesial Repentance*, p. 208.

21 Fredriksen, *Sin*, p. 148.

22 D. Bonhoeffer, *Life Together* (new edition) (London: SCM Press, 2015), p. 86.

23 F. Spufford, *Unapologetic: Why, despite everything, Christianity can still make surprising emotional sense* (London: Faber and Faber, 2012), p. 27.

24 T. H. Warren, 'We're all sinners, and accepting that is actually a good thing', *New York Times* (6 March 2022), <www.nytimes.com/2022/03/06/opinion/sin-lent-grace -forgiveness.html?smtyp=cur&smid=tw-nytopinion> (accessed 15 August 2022).

25 Bonhoeffer, *Life Together*, p. 68.

26 Portmann, *A History of Sin*, p. 177.

27 McFarland, 'Original sin', p. 318.

28 Konstan, *The Origin of Sin*, p. 68.

29 D. Bonhoeffer, *The Cost of Discipleship* (London: SCM Press, 2015), p. 212.

30 D. Willard, *Renovation of the Heart* (Colorado Springs, CO: NavPress, 2002), p. 226.

31 D. Willard, *The Great Omission: Reclaiming Jesus's essential teachings on discipleship* (Oxford: Monarch, 2009), p. 150.

32 J. K. A. Smith, *Desiring the Kingdom: Worship, worldview, and cultural formation*, Cultural Liturgies (Grand Rapids, MI: Baker Academic, 2009), p. 51.

33 Augustine (R. S. Pine-Coffin, trans.), *Confessions* (London: Penguin, 1961), 1.1.1.

34 Willard, *The Great Omission*, pp. 85–86.

35 S. Ray, 'Structural sin', in K. L. Johnson and D. Lauber (eds), *T&T Clark Companion to the Doctrine of Sin*, (London: Bloomsbury T&T Clark, 2018), pp. 417–32 and 417.

36 Ray, 'Structural sin', p. 417.

37 W. J. Jennings, *The Christian Imagination: Theology and the origins of race* (New Haven, CT: Yale University Press, 2010), p. 9.

38 J. H. Cone, *A Black Theology of Liberation* (Maryknoll, NY: Orbis, 1990), p. 113.

39 J. H. Cone, *God of the Oppressed* (Maryknoll, NY: Orbis, 1997), p. 28.

40 Cone, *A Black Theology of Liberation*, p. 63.

41 Bergen, *Ecclesial Repentance*, p. 190.

42 Bergen, *Ecclesial Repentance*, p. 191.

43 C. H. Spurgeon, *The Quotable Spurgeon* (Wheaton, IL: H. Shaw, 1990), p. 75.

4 The failing Church

1 J. Rebanks, *English Pastoral: An inheritance* (London: Penguin, 2021), p. 13.

2 W. J. Jennings, *The Christian Imagination: Theology and origins of race* (New Haven, CT: Yale University Press, 2010), p. 291.

3 J. R. D. Kirk, 'Principalities and powers', in K. L. Johnson and D. Lauber (eds), *T&T Clark Companion to the Doctrine of Sin* (London: Bloomsbury T&T Clark, 2018), p. 402.

4 S. Ray, 'Structural sin', in K. L. Johnson and D. Lauber (eds), *T&T Clark Companion to the Doctrine of Sin* (London: Bloomsbury T&T Clark, 2018), p. 426.

5 W. Wink, *The Powers that Be: Theology for a new millennium* (New York: Bantam Doubleday Dell, 2000), p. 189.

6 Kirk, 'Principalities and powers', p. 404.

7 R. W. Jenson, *Systematic Theology: Volume II: The works of God* (Oxford: Oxford University Press, 1999), p. 173.

8 J. J. Navone, *Triumph through Failure: A theology of the cross* (Eugene, OR: Wipf & Stock, 1984), p. 138.

9 P. Oakes, *Galatians,* Paideia Commentaries on the New Testament (Grand Rapids, MI: Baker Academic, 2015), p. 176.

10 I am grateful to Dr Isabelle Hamley for these insights from a Bible study she shared with the bishops of the Church of England at a residential retreat.

11 F. F. Bruce, *The Epistle to the Galatians: A commentary on the Greek text* (Exeter: Paternoster Press, 1982), p. 248.

12 Wink, *The Powers that Be*, p.171.

13 Bruce, *The Epistle to the Galatians*, p. 249.

14 Faith and Order Commission of the Church of England/ Living in Love and Faith, *Friendship and the Body of Christ: A Living in Love and Faith resource for reflection and conversation* (London: Church House Publishing, 2022), p. 39.

15 Faith and Order Commission, *Friendship and the Body of Christ*, p. 42.

16 Bruce, *The Epistle to the Galatians*, p. 249.

17 Church of England, 'Vision and strategy: A vision and strategy for the Church of England in the 2020s', Church of England (n.d.), <www.churchofengland.org/about /leadership-and-governance/emerging-church-england /vision-and-strategy> (accessed 15 June 2022).

18 S. Cottrell, 'Vision and strategy address, General Synod November 2021', The Archbishop of York, The Church of

England (17 November 2021), <www.archbishopofyork
.org/speaking-and-writing/sermons/vision-and-strategy
-address-general-synod-november-2021> (accessed 15 June
2022).

19 L. McFerran and L. Graveling, 'Clergy in a time of Covid:
Autonomy, accountability and support, Panel Survey
Wave 3', Living Ministry, The Church of England (January
2022), <www.churchofengland.org/sites/default/files/2022
-01/Living%20Ministry%20W3%20Panel%20Survey
%20Report%20-%20Clergy%20in%20a%20Time%20of
%20Covid_0.pdf> (accessed 2 September 2022).

20 G. Francis-Dehqani, 'Diocesan Synod June 2022,
Presidential Address by the Bishop of Chelmsford', The
Church of England in Essex and East London, Diocese of
Chelmsford (11 June 2022), <www.chelmsford.anglican
.org/news/article/diocesan-synod-june-2022-presidential
-address-by-the-bishop-of-chelmsford> (accessed 17
August 2022).

21 R. Rumelt, *Good Strategy, Bad Strategy: The difference and
why it matters* (London: Profile Books, 2012), p. 9.

22 D. Bonhoeffer, *Life Together* (new edition) (London: SCM
Press, 2015), p. 16.

23 Navone, *Triumph through Failure*, p. 122.

24 E. Katongole, *Mirror to the Church: Resurrecting faith
after genocide in Rwanda* (Grand Rapids, MI: Zondervan,
2009), p. 145.

25 Katongole, *Mirror to the Church*, p. 147.

26 See also John 2.4; 6.6; 8.14;13.3 and 19.28.

27 M. Heffernan, *Uncharted: How uncertainty can power
change* (London: Simon & Schuster, 2020), p. 79.

28 Heffernan, *Uncharted*, p. 339.

29 J. Moran, *If You Should Fail: A book of solace* (London: Penguin Random House, 2021), p. 14.

30 L. Alexander and M. Higton (eds), *Faithful Improvisation? Theological reflections on church leadership* (London: Church House Publishing, 2016), p. 84.

31 E. Ineson, *Ambition: What Jesus said about power, success and counting stuff* (London: SPCK, 2019), p. 19.

32 J. Hindley, '"I can't afford to fail": The testimony of a bad church planter', Union (n.d.), <www.uniontheology.org/resources/doctrine/sin-and-evil/i-cant-afford-to-fail-the-testimony-of-a-bad-church-planter> (accessed 17 August 2022).

33 P. Bradbury, 'Beyond measure', His Light Material (7 April 2022), <https://hislightmaterial.wordpress.com/2022/04/07/beyond-measure> (accessed 17 August 2022).

34 J. R. Briggs, *Fail: Finding hope and grace in the midst of ministry failure* (Downers Grove, IL: InterVarsity Press, 2014), p. 73.

35 Pope Francis, 'Vespers with priests and religious: Homily of His Holiness Pope Francis, St Patrick's Cathedral, New York', Vatican (24 September 2015), <www.vatican.va/content/francesco/en/homilies/2015/documents/papa-francesco_20150924_usa-omelia-vespri-nyc.html> (accessed 18 August 2022).

36 P. Bradbury, '50 words for "church"', His Light Material (31 May 2022), <https://hislightmaterial.wordpress.com/2022/05> (accessed 17 June 2022).

37 Rebanks, *English Pastoral*, p. 254.

38 Rebanks, *English Pastoral*, p. 252.

39 See, for example, S. Aisthorpe, *Rewilding the Church* (Edinburgh: Saint Andrew Press, 2020).

40 G. Rust, 'Church is a verb', Wordsout (2003), <www .wordsout.co.uk/church_is_a_verb.htm> (accessed 12 October 2022). © Godfrey Rust, <www.wordsout.co.uk>. Reproduced by permission of Godfrey Rust.

41 'Archbishop of Canterbury gives final Keynote Address at the Lambeth Conference', The Archbishop of Canterbury, The Church of England (7 August 2022), <www.archbishopofcanterbury.org/speaking-writing /speeches/archbishop-canterbury-gives-final-keynote -address-lambeth-conference> (accessed 6 September 2022).

42 Rebanks, *English Pastoral*, p. 267.

5 The greatest failure of all

1 K. Bailey, *The Good Shepherd: A thousand-year journey from psalm 23 to the New Testament* (London: SPCK, 2015), p. 57.

2 J. Houston, M. Crocker and S. Lighthelm, 'Oceans (Where feet may fail)' (Reloaded) (audio), lyrics © Capitol Christian Music Group.

3 R. Parker, *Free to Fail* (London: Triangle, 1998), p. 59.

4 W. Willimon, *Listeners Dare: Hearing God in the sermon* (Nashville, TN: Abingdon, 2022), p. 76.

5 J. J. Navone, *Triumph through Failure: A theology of the cross* (Eugene, OR: Wipf & Stock, 1984), p. 25 (italics mine).

6 Parker, *Free to Fail*, p. 71.

7 J. Calvin (H. Beveridge, trans.), *Institutes of the Christian Religion* (Peabody, MA: Hendrickson, 2009), 2.16.10.

8 Acts 2.31; Ephesians 4.8–10; 1 Peter 3.18–20.

9 Irenaeus (A. Roberts, trans.) *Against Heresies* (Jackson, MI: Ex Fontibus Company, 2017), 4.27.

10 Thomas Aquinas, *Summa Theologiae*, New Advent, <www.newadvent.org/summa/4052.htm> (accessed 25 August 2022), 3.52. I am grateful to Dr Justin Stratis for the insights into the harrowing of hell in his blog entry, 'Did Jesus descend into hell?', Trinity College Bristol (n.d.), <www.trinitycollegebristol.ac.uk/blog/kingdom-learning/did-jesus-descend-into-hell> (accessed 25 August 2022).

11 S. Rambo, 'The hell of Holy Saturday', The Christian Century (7 April 2020), <www.christiancentury.org/blog-post/guest-post/hell-holy-saturday> (accessed 25 August 2022).

12 H. U. von Balthasar (G. Harrison, trans.), *Theo-Drama: Volume III: The dramatis personae: Persons in Christ* (San Francisco, CA: Ignatius Press, 1978), pp. 238–9.

13 H. U. von Balthasar (A. Nichols, trans.), *Mysterium Paschale: The mystery of Easter* (Edinburgh: T&T Clark, Edinburgh/San Francisco, CA: Ignatius Press, 2000), p. 174.

14 Rambo, 'The hell of Holy Saturday'.

15 D. Ford, *The Gospel of John: A theological commentary* (Grand Rapids, MI: Baker Academic, 2022), p. 318.

16 See also Matthew 17.22–23; 20.17–19; Mark 8.31–32; 9.30–32; 10.32–34; Luke 9.21–22; 18.31–34.

17 G. Francis-Dehqani, G. James, M. Oakley and M. Whipp, *Reflections for Lent 2021: 17 February–3 April 2021* (London: Church House, 2020), p. 47.

18 R. McLauchlan, *Saturday's Silence: R. S. Thomas and paschal reading* (Cardiff: University of Wales Press, 2016), p. 1.

19 R. S. Thomas, *Not that He Brought Flowers* (London: Rupert Hart-Davis, 1968), p. 32. (© Bloodaxe Books, R. S. Thomas, *Selected Poems 1946–1968*, Bloodaxe Books, 1986.)

20 'Easter Saturday' is another term for 'Holy Saturday'.

21 A. E. Lewis, *Between Cross and Resurrection: A theology of Holy Saturday* (Grand Rapids, MI: William B. Eerdmans, 2003), p. 341.

22 P. Greig, *God on Mute: Engaging the silence of unanswered prayer* (Eastbourne: David C. Cook, 2007), p. 239.

23 Rambo 'The hell of Holy Saturday'.

24 K. L. Johnson, 'He descended into hell', Institute for Faith and Learning, Baylor University (2014), <www.baylor.edu/content/services/document.php/217609> (accessed 27 August 2022).

25 Thomas, *Not that He Brought Flowers*, p. 32. (© Bloodaxe Books, R. S. Thomas, *Selected Poems 1946–1968*, Bloodaxe Books, 1986.)

26 Navone, *Triumph through Failure*, p. 183.

27 McLaughlin, *Saturday's Silence*, p. 126.

28 Lewis, *Between Cross and Resurrection*, p. 466.

6 How to fail really well

1 The School of Life, *On Failure: How to succeed at defeat* (London: The School of Life, 2022), p. 130.

2 J. Portmann, *A History of Sin: Its evolution to today and beyond: How evil changes, but never goes away* (Lanham, MD: Rowman & Littlefield, 2007), p. 179.

3 S. H. Kellert, *In the Wake of Chaos: Unpredictable order in dynamical systems* (Chicago, IL: University of Chicago Press, 1993), p. 2.

4 A. Kuyper, 'Inaugural address at the dedication of the Free University', in J. D. Bratt (ed.), *Abraham Kuyper: A centennial reader* (Grand Rapids, MI: Eerdmans, 1998), p. 488.

5 Save the Parish: <https://savetheparish.com>.

6 J. L. Zecher, 'Acedia: the lost name for the emotion we're all feeling right now', The Conversation (27 August 2020), <www.theconversation.com/acedia-the-lost-name-for-the -emotion-were-all-feeling-right-now-144058> (accessed 15 June 2022).

7 Thomas Aquinas, *Summa Theologiae*, New Advent, <www .newadvent.org/summa/3035.htm> (accessed 25 August 2022), 2.35.

8 J. Cassian (B. Ramsay, trans.), *The Institutes*, Ancient Christian Writers No. 58 (New York: The Newman Press, 2000), p. 217.

9 K. Norris, *Acedia and Me: A marriage, monks, and a writer's life* (New York: Riverhead Books, 2010), p. 3.

10 J. Moran, *If You Should Fail: A book of solace* (London: Penguin Random House, 2021), p. 133.

11 Quoted in C. Tavris and E. Aronson, *Mistakes Were Made (but Not by Me): Why we justify foolish beliefs, bad decisions and hurtful acts* (London: Pinter & Martin, 2020), p. 315.

12 Moran, *If You Should Fail*, p.13.

13 William Shakespeare, *King Lear*, I.i.

14 Aristotle, *Poetics* (revised edition) (London: Penguin, 1996), p. 21.

15 For example, Movers and Shakespeares: <www .moversandshakespeares.com>.

16 G. Jones and K. C. Armstrong, *Resurrecting Excellence: Shaping faithful Christian ministry* (Grand Rapids, MI: Eerdmans, 2006), p. 65.

17 Tavris and Aronson, *Mistakes Were Made*, p. 304.

18 C. S Lewis, *The Four Loves* (London: William Collins, 2012), p. 78. *The Four Loves* by C. S. Lewis © copyright 1960 CS Lewis Pte Ltd. Reproduced by permission.

19 Tavris and Aronson, *Mistakes Were Made*, p. 305.

20 S. Salai, 'Pope Francis and the theology of failure: Q&A with John Navone, S.J.', *America: The Jesuit Review of Faith & Culture* (15 June 2016), <www.americamagazine .org/content/all-things/pope-francis-and-theology-failure -12-questions-john-navone-sj> (accessed 12 April 2022).

21 Church of England, 'An order for night prayer (compline) in traditional language', *Common Worship: Daily Prayer* (5 March 2019), <https://daily.commonworship.com/daily.cgi ?today_np=1&book=bcp> (accessed 30 August 2022).

22 S. Pinker, 'Three ways to be more rational this year', BBC News online (1 January 2022), <www.bbc.co.uk/news /world-59740588> (accessed 30 August 2022).

23 The School of Life, *On Failure*, p. 178.

24 C. M. Christensen, *The Innovator's Dilemma: When new technologies cause great firms to fail* (Boston, MA: Harvard Business Review Press, 2016), p. 234.

25 J. Hindley, '"I can't afford to fail": The testimony of a bad

church planter', Union (n.d.), <www.uniontheology.org /resources/doctrine/sin-and-evil/i-cant-afford-to-fail-the -testimony-of-a-bad-church-planter> (accessed 17 August 2022).

26 J. J. Navone, *Triumph through Failure: A theology of the cross* (Eugene, OR: Wipf & Stock, 1984), p. 182.

27 Shakespeare, *Measure for Measure*, I.v.

28 Shakespeare, *King Lear*, I.iv.

29 Shakespeare, *Twelfth Night*, I.v.

30 T. Eagleton, *Humour* (New Haven, CT: Yale University Press, 2022), p. 163.

31 T. Almeida and C. Josten, 'Not a joke: leveraging humour at work increases performance, individual happiness, and psychological safety', LSE blog (28 April 2021), <https:// blogs.lse.ac.uk/businessreview/2021/04/28/not-a-joke -leveraging-humour-at-work-increases-performance -individual-happiness-and-psychological-safety> (accessed 28 August 2022).

32 Portmann, *A History of Sin*, p. 181.

Bibliography

Aisthorpe, S., *Rewilding the Church* (Edinburgh: Saint
  Andrew Press, 2020).

Alexander, L. and Higton, M. (eds), *Faithful Improvisation?*
  Theological Reflections on Church Leadership (London:
  Church House Publishing, 2016).

Almeida, T. and Josten, C., 'Not a joke: leveraging humour
  at work increases performance, individual happiness, and
  psychological safety', LSE blog (28 April 2021), <https://
  blogs.lse.ac.uk/businessreview/2021/04/28/not-a-joke
  -leveraging-humour-at-work-increases-performance
  -individual-happiness-and-psychological-safety> (accessed
  28 August 2022).

Aquinas, T., *Summa Theologiae*, New Advent, <www
  .newadvent.org/summa/4052.htm> (accessed 25 August
  2022).

Archbishop of Canterbury, News, 'Archbishop of Canterbury
  apologises to Indigenous peoples of Canada', The
  Archbishop of Canterbury, The Church of England (2 May
  2022), <www.archbishopofcanterbury.org/news/news-and
  -statements/archbishop-canterbury-apologises-indigenous
  -peoples-canada> (accessed 12 October 2022).

Archbishop of Canterbury, 'Archbishop of Canterbury
  gives final Keynote Address at the Lambeth Conference',
  The Archbishop of Canterbury, The Church of England
  (7 August 2022), <www.archbishopofcanterbury.org
  /speaking-writing/speeches/archbishop-canterbury-gives

-final-keynote-address-lambeth-conference> (accessed 6 September 2022).

Archbishops' Anti-Racism Taskforce, 'From lament to action: The report of the Archbishops' Anti-Racism Taskforce (London: Church of England), <www.churchofengland.org /sites/default/files/2021-04/FromLamentToAction-report .pdf> (accessed 20 May 2022).

Aristotle, *Poetics* (revised edition) (London: Penguin, 1996).

Augustine (H. Bettenson, trans.), *City of God* (London: Penguin, 1972).

Augustine (R. S. Pine-Coffin, trans.), *Confessions* (London: Penguin, 1961).

Bailey, K., *The Good Shepherd: A thousand-year journey from psalm 23 to the New Testament* (London: SPCK, 2015).

Balthasar, H. U. von (A. Nichols, trans.), *Mysterium Paschale: The mystery of Easter* (Edinburgh: T&T Clark, Edinburgh/ San Francisco, CA: Ignatius Press, 2000).

Balthasar, H. U. von (G. Harrison, trans.), *Theo-Drama: Volume III: The dramatis personae: Persons in Christ* (San Francisco, CA: Ignatius Press, 1978).

Basil the Great, St, *Detailed Rule for Monks* (resp. 2.1: PG 31.908–910), quoted in J. Portmann, *A History of Sin: Its evolution to today and beyond: How evil changes, but never goes away* (Lanham, MD: Rowman & Littlefield, 2007).

Beckett, S., *Company / Ill Seen Ill Said / Worstward Ho / Stirrings Still* (London: Faber and Faber, 2009).

Beresford, S., *The Southbury Child,* NHB Modern Plays (London: Nick Hern Books, 2022).

Bergen, J. M., *Ecclesial Repentance: The churches confront their sinful pasts* (London: T&T Clark, 2011).

Black, C. C., 'Synoptic Gospels', in K. L. Johnson and D. Lauber (eds), *T&T Clark Companion to the Doctrine of Sin* (London: Bloomsbury T&T Clark, 2018).

Bonhoeffer, D., *The Cost of Discipleship* (London: SCM Press, 2015).

Bonhoeffer, D. (C. Green, ed.), *Ethics*, Dietrich Bonhoeffer Works (Minneapolis, MN: Augsburg Fortress Press, 2009).

Bonhoeffer, D., *Life Together* (new edition) (London: SCM Press, 2015).

Bradbury, P., '50 words for "church"', His Light Material (31 May 2022), <https://hislightmaterial.wordpress.com /2022/05> (accessed 17 June 2022).

Bradbury, P., 'Beyond measure', His Light Material (7 April 2022), <https://hislightmaterial.wordpress.com/2022/04/07 /beyond-measure> (accessed 17 August 2022).

Bratt (ed.), J. D., *Abraham Kuyper: A centennial reader* (Grand Rapids, MI: Eerdmans, 1998).

Briggs, J. R., *Fail: Finding hope and grace in the midst of ministry failure* (Downers Grove, IL: InterVarsity Press, 2014).

Brown, B., quoted in J. R. Briggs, *Fail: Finding hope and grace in the midst of ministry failure* (Downers Grove, IL: InterVarsity Press, 2014).

Brown, B., *The Gifts of Imperfection* (London: Vermilion, 2020).

Bruce, F. F. *The Epistle to the Galatians: A commentary on the Greek text* (Exeter: Paternoster Press, 1982).

Buechner, F., *Beyond Words: Daily readings in the ABC's of faith* (San Francisco, CA: HarperSanFrancisco, 2004).

Calvin, J. (H. Beveridge, trans.), *Institutes of the Christian Religion* (Peabody, MA: Hendrickson, 2009).

Cambridge Dictionary online, <https://dictionary.cambridge
.org/dictionary/english/failure> (accessed 3 September
2022).

Cassian, J. (B. Ramsay, trans.),*The Institutes*, Ancient
Christian Writers No. 58 (New York: The Newman Press,
2000).

Christensen, C. M., *The Innovator's Dilemma: When new
technologies cause great firms to fail* (Boston, MA: Harvard
Business Review Press, 2016).

Church Commissioners for England, 'Church
Commissioners' research into historic links to transatlantic
chattel slavery', The Church of England (June 2022), <www
.churchofengland.org/sites/default/files/2022-06/Church
%20Commissioners%20research%20report%20final.pdf>
(accessed 21 August 2022).

Church of England, 'A commination or denouncing of
God's anger and judgements against sinners', Book of
Common Prayer, The Church of England (n.d.), <www
.churchofengland.org/prayer-and-worship/worship-texts
-and-resources/book-common-prayer/commination>
(accessed 12 October 2022).

Church of England, 'An order for night prayer (compline) in
traditional language', *Common Worship: Daily Prayer* (5
March 2019), <https://daily.commonworship.com/daily.cgi
?today_np=1&book=bcp> (accessed 30 August 2022).

Church of England, 'Vision and strategy: A vision and
strategy for the Church of England in the 2020s', Church
of England (n.d.), <www.churchofengland.org/about
/leadership-and-governance/emerging-church-england
/vision-and-strategy>, accessed 15 June 2022).

Community of the Cross of Nails, 'Growing together in hope' (n.d.), <www.coventrycathedral.org.uk/uploads/media /Coventry-Cross-of-Nails-Oct-19-HI-RES.pdf> (accessed 12 October 2022).

Cone, J. H., *A Black Theology of Liberation* (Maryknoll, NY: Orbis, 1990).

Cone, J. H., *God of the Oppressed* (Maryknoll, NY: Orbis, 1997).

Cottrell, S., 'Vision and strategy address, General Synod November 2021', The Archbishop of York, The Church of England (17 November 2021), <www.archbishopofyork .org/speaking-and-writing/sermons/vision-and-strategy -address-general-synod-november-2021> (accessed 15 June 2022).

Day, E. *Failosophy: A handbook for when things go wrong* (London: HarperCollins, 2020).

Day, E., *How to Fail: Everything I've ever learned from things going wrong* (London: HarperCollins, 2019).

Eagleton, T., *Humour* (New Haven, CT: Yale University Press, 2022).

Edmondson, A., *The Fearless Organization: Creating psychological safety in the workplace for learning, innovation, and growth* (Hoboken, NJ: John Wiley, 2019).

Edmondson, A. C., 'Strategies for learning from failure', *Harvard Business Review* magazine (April 2011), <https:// hbr.org/2011/04/strategies-for-learning-from-failure> (accessed 1 September 2022).

Faith and Order Commission of the Church of England/ Living in Love and Faith, *Friendship and the Body of Christ: A Living in Love and Faith resource for reflection and conversation* (London: Church House Publishing, 2022).

Feltham, C., *Failure* (London: Routledge, 2012).

Ford, D., *The Gospel of John: A theological commentary* (Grand Rapids, MI: Baker Academic, 2022).

Francis, Pope, 'Vespers with priests and religious: Homily of His Holiness Pope Francis, St Patrick's Cathedral, New York', Vatican (24 September 2015), <www.vatican .va/content/francesco/en/homilies/2015/documents/papa -francesco_20150924_usa-omelia-vespri-nyc.html> (accessed 18 August 2022).

Francis-Dehqani, G., 'Diocesan Synod June 2022, Presidential Address by the Bishop of Chelmsford', The Church of England in Essex and East London, Diocese of Chelmsford (11 June 2022), <www.chelmsford.anglican.org/news /article/diocesan-synod-june-2022-presidential-address-by -the-bishop-of-chelmsford> (accessed 17 August 2022).

Francis-Dehqani, G., James, G., Oakley, M. and Whipp, M., *Reflections for Lent 2021: 17 February–3 April 2021* (London: Church House, 2020).

Fredriksen, P., *Sin: The early history of an idea* (Princeton, NJ: Princeton University Press, 2012).

Gorman, A. *The Hill We Climb: An inaugural poem for the country* (London: Chatto & Windus, 2021).

Greig, P., *God on Mute: Engaging the silence of unanswered prayer* (Eastbourne: David C. Cook, 2007).

Headteacher, quoted in M. Syed, *Black Box Thinking: Marginal gains and the secrets of high performance* (London: John Murray, 2016).

Health and Safety Executive, 'Leadership and worker

involvement toolkit', Health and Safety Executive (n.d.),
<www.hse.gov.uk/construction/lwit/index.htm> (accessed
4 September 2022).

Heffernan, M., *Uncharted: How uncertainty can power change*
(London: Simon & Schuster, 2020).

Himid, L., 'The art of failure', Tate (3 October 2018), <www
.tate.org.uk/art/artists/lubaina-himid-2356/art-failure>
(accessed 5 September 2022).

Hindley, J., '"I can't afford to fail": The testimony of a bad
church planter', Union (n.d.), <www.uniontheology.org
/resources/doctrine/sin-and-evil/i-cant-afford-to-fail-the
-testimony-of-a-bad-church-planter> (accessed 17 August
2022).

Houston, J., Crocker, M. and Lighthelm, S., 'Oceans (Where
feet may fail)' (Reloaded) (audio), lyrics © Capitol
Christian Music Group.

Ineson, E., *Ambition: What Jesus said about power, success
and counting stuff* (London: SPCK, 2019).

Irenaeus (A. Roberts, trans.) *Against Heresies* (Jackson, MI:
Ex Fontibus Company, 2017).

Jennings, W. J., *The Christian Imagination: Theology and the
origins of race* (New Haven, CT: Yale University Press,
2010).

Jenson, R. W., *Systematic Theology: Volume II: The works of
God* (Oxford: Oxford University Press, 1999).

Johnson, K. L., 'He descended into hell', Institute for Faith
and Learning, Baylor University (2014), <www.baylor.edu
/content/services/document.php/217609> (accessed 27
August 2022).

Johnson, K. L. and Lauber, D. (eds), *T&T Clark Companion*

to the Doctrine of Sin (London: Bloomsbury T&T Clark, 2018).

Jones, G. and Armstrong, K. C., *Resurrecting Excellence: Shaping faithful Christian ministry* (Grand Rapids, MI: Eerdmans, 2006).

Jowett, J., Montgomery, W., Taylor, G. and Wells, S. (eds), *The Oxford Shakespeare: The complete works* (second edition), (Oxford: Clarendon Press, 2005).

Katongole, E., *Mirror to the Church: Resurrecting faith after genocide in Rwanda* (Grand Rapids, MI: Zondervan, 2009).

Kellert, S. H., *In the Wake of Chaos: Unpredictable order in dynamical systems* (Chicago, IL: University of Chicago Press, 1993).

Kirk, J. R. D. 'Principalities and powers', in K. L. Johnson and D. Lauber (eds), *T&T Clark Companion to the Doctrine of Sin*, (London: Bloomsbury T&T Clark, 2018).

Konstan, D., *The Origin of Sin: Greece and Rome, early Judaism and Christianity* (London: Bloomsbury Academic, 2022).

Kuyper, A., 'Inaugural address at the dedication of the Free University', in J. D. Bratt (ed.), *Abraham Kuyper: A centennial reader* (Grand Rapids, MI: Eerdmans, 1998).

Lambeth Conference, 'Lambeth Calls', Lambeth Conference (July 2022) <www.lambethconference.org/wp-content /uploads/2022/07/Lambeth-Calls-July-2022.pdf> (accessed 14 October 2022).

Lewis, A. E., *Between Cross and Resurrection: A theology of Holy Saturday* (Grand Rapids, MI: William B. Eerdmans, 2003).

Lewis, C. S., *The Four Loves* (London: William Collins, 2012).

Liturgy Office, England and Wales, 'Rite of penance: Introduction', excerpts from the Rite of Penance 1974, 1975, International Commission on English in the Liturgy Inc. (London: Liturgy Office, England and Wales, 1975), <www.liturgyoffice.org.uk/Resources/Penance/Penance-Intro.pdf> (accessed 14 August 2022).

McDermott, J., 'Feel like you've failed this Lent? Maybe that's the point', *America: The Jesuit Review of Faith & Culture* (5 April 2022), <www.americamagazine.org/faith/2022/04/05/lent-resolution-failure-242760> (accessed 5 September 2022).

McFarland, I. A., 'Original sin', in K. L. Johnson and D. Lauber (eds), *T&T Clark Companion to the Doctrine of Sin* (London: Bloomsbury T&T Clark, 2018).

McFerran, L. and Graveling, L., 'Clergy in a time of Covid: Autonomy, accountability and support, Panel Survey Wave 3', Living Ministry, The Church of England (January 2022), <www.churchofengland.org/sites/default/files/2022-01/Living%20Ministry%20W3%20Panel%20Survey%20Report%20-%20Clergy%20in%20a%20Time%20of%20Covid_0.pdf> (accessed 2 September 2022).

McLauchlan, R., *Saturday's Silence: R. S. Thomas and paschal reading* (Cardiff: University of Wales Press, 2016).

Maxwell, J. C., *Failing Forward: Turning mistakes into stepping stones for success* (Nashville, TN: Thomas Nelson, 2000).

Meierhans, J., 'Archbishop of Canterbury says his faith helped during depression', BBC News online (20 February 2022), <www.bbc.co.uk/news/uk-60451794> (accessed 12 October 2022).

Mertens, U, from *THE FOCUS*, and John J. Grumbar, from
Egon Zehnder, London, 'Interview with Archbishop
Desmond Tutu', Egon Zehnder (1 January 2017), <www
.egonzehnder.com/insight/interview-with-archbishop
-desmond-tutu> (accessed 7 October 2022).

Mills, M., '"We had such trust, we feel such fools": How
shocking hospital mistakes led to our daughter's death',
The Guardian online (3 September 2022), <www
.theguardian.com/lifeandstyle/2022/sep/03/13-year-old
-daughter-dead-in-five-weeks-hospital-mistakes?CMP=
Share_iOSApp_Other> (accessed 3 September 2022).

Moran, J., *If You Should Fail: A book of solace* (London:
Penguin Random House, 2021).

Navone, J. J., *Triumph through Failure: A theology of the cross*
(Eugene, OR: Wipf & Stock, 1984).

Norris, K., *Acedia and Me: A marriage, monks, and a writer's
life* (New York: Riverhead Books, 2010).

Oakes, P., *Galatians,* Paideia Commentaries on the New
Testament (Grand Rapids, MI: Baker Academic, 2015).

Oxford Learner's Dictionaries online, <www
.oxfordlearnersdictionaries.com/definition/english/failure>
(accessed 3 September 2022).

Parker, R., *Free to Fail* (London: Triangle, 1998).

Pinker, S., 'Three ways to be more rational this year', BBC
News online (1 January 2022), <www.bbc.co.uk/news
/world-59740588> (accessed 30 August 2022).

Portmann, J., *A History of Sin: Its evolution to today and
beyond: How evil changes, but never goes away* (Lanham,
MD: Rowman & Littlefield, 2007).

Rambo, S., 'The hell of Holy Saturday', The Christian

Century (7 April 2020), <www.christiancentury.org/blog
-post/guest-post/hell-holy-saturday> (accessed 25 August
2022).

Ray, S., 'Structural sin', in K. L. Johnson and D. Lauber (eds),
T&T Clark Companion to the Doctrine of Sin (London:
Bloomsbury T&T Clark, 2018).

Rebanks, R., *English Pastoral: An inheritance* (London:
Penguin, 2020).

Rumelt, R., *Good Strategy, Bad Strategy: The difference and
why it matters* (London: Profile Books, 2012).

Rust, G., 'Church is a verb', Wordsout (2003), <www
.wordsout.co.uk/church_is_a_verb.htm> (accessed 12
October 2022).

Salai, S., 'Pope Francis and the theology of failure: Q&A
with John Navone, S.J.', *America: The Jesuit Review of
Faith & Culture* (15 June 2016), <www.americamagazine
.org/content/all-things/pope-francis-and-theology-failure
-12-questions-john-navone-sj> (accessed 12 April 2022).

Sayer, M., *A Non-anxious Presence: How a changing and
complex world will create a remnant of renewed Christian
leaders* (Chicago, IL: Moody 2022).

School of Life, The, *On Failure: How to succeed at defeat*
(London: The School of Life, 2022).

Smith, J. K. A., *Desiring the Kingdom: Worship, worldview,
and cultural formation*, Cultural Liturgies (Grand Rapids,
MI: Baker Academic, 2009).

Solzhenitsyn, A. (T. P. Whitney and H. Willetts, trans.),
*The Gulag Archipelago 1918–56: An experiment in literary
investigation* (abridged) (London: Vintage, 2018).

Spufford, F., *Unapologetic: Why, despite everything,*

Christianity can still make surprising emotional sense
(London: Faber and Faber, 2012).

Spurgeon, C. H., *The Quotable Spurgeon* (Wheaton, IL: H.
Shaw, 1990).

Syed, M., *Black Box Thinking: Marginal gains and the secrets
of high performance* (London: John Murray, 2016).

Tavris, C. and Aronson, E., *Mistakes Were Made (but Not
by Me): Why we justify foolish beliefs, bad decisions and
hurtful acts* (London: Pinter & Martin, 2020).

Thomas, R. S., *Not that He Brought Flowers* (London: Rupert
Hart-Davis, 1968).

Tristram, Brother, *Exciting Holiness: Collects and readings for
the festivals and lesser festivals of the calendar of the Church
of England* (Norwich: Canterbury Press, 2007).

Vanderheiden, E. and Mayer, C.-H. (eds), *Mistakes, Errors
and Failures across Cultures: Navigating potentials* (Cham,
Switzerland: Springer, 2020).

Warren, T., 'We're all sinners, and accepting that is
actually a good thing', *New York Times* (6 March 2022),
<www.nytimes.com/2022/03/06/opinion/sin-lent-grace
-forgiveness.html?smtyp=cur&smid=tw-nytopinion>
(accessed 15 August 2022).

Willard, D., *The Great Omission: Reclaiming Jesus's essential
teachings on discipleship* (Oxford: Monarch, 2009).

Willard, D., *Renovation of the Heart* (Colorado Springs, CO:
NavPress, 2002).

Willimon, W., *Listeners Dare: Hearing God in the sermon*
(Nashville, TN: Abingdon, 2022).

Wink, W., *The Powers that Be: Theology for a new millennium*
(New York: Bantam Doubleday Dell, 2000).

Zecher, J. L., 'Acedia: the lost name for the emotion we're all feeling right now', The Conversation (27 August 2020), <www.theconversation.com/acedia-the-lost-name-for-the-emotion-were-all-feeling-right-now-144058> (accessed 15 June 2022).

Zull, J. E., *From Brain to Mind: Using neuroscience to guide change in education* (Sterling, VA: Stylus, 2011).

The Big Church Read

Did you know that you can read

Failure

as a Big Church Read?

Join together with friends, your small group
or your whole church, or do it on your own,
as Emma Ineson leads you through the book.

Visit www.thebigchurchread.co.uk or use the QR code below
to watch exclusive videos from Emma Ineson
as she explores the ideas and themes of *Failure*.

The Big Church Read will also provide you with a reading plan
and discussion questions to help guide you through the book.

It's free to join in and a great way to read through
Failure!